To "Sta

From "b

Enjoy !

Cigars, Whiskey & Winning

LEADERSHIP LESSONS

from

GENERAL ULYSSES S. GRANT

AL KALTMAN

PRENTICE HALL PRESS

Library of Congress Cataloging-in-Publication Data

Kaltman, Al.
    Cigars, whiskey, and winning : leadership lessons from
General Ulysses S. Grant / Al Kaltman.
        p. cm.
    Includes index.
    ISBN 0-7352-0022-X
    1. Leadership. 2. Grant, Ulysses S. (Ulysses Simpson), 1822-1885.
3. Generals—United States—Biography. I. Title.
HD57.7.K357   1998
658.4—dc21   98-25269
                                                          CIP

© 1998 by Prentice Hall

Printed in the United States of America.

10 9 8 7 6 5 4 3 2 1

ISBN 0-7352-0022-X

PRENTICE HALL PRESS
Paramus, NJ 07652

A Simon & Schuster Company

On the World Wide Web at http://www.phdirect.com

Prentice Hall International (UK) Limited, *London*
Prentice Hall of Australia Pty. Limited, *Sydney*
Prentice Hall Canada Inc., *Toronto*
Prentice Hall Hispanoamericana, S.A., *Mexico*
Prentice Hall of India Private Limited, *New Delhi*
Prentice Hall of Japan, *Tokyo*
Simon & Schuster Asia Pte. Ltd., *Singapore*
Editora Prentice-Hall do Brasil, Ltda., *Rio de Janeiro*

TO GWEN

ACKNOWLEDGMENTS

The second luckiest day of my life was the day I met Jack Byrne. Much of what I know about management I learned from him at the Travelers, GEICO, Merastar, and Fund American. I am forever in his debt.

The luckiest day of my life was when I met my wife, Gwen. An excellent manager, she reviewed every word I wrote, challenging the content and the presentation of the lessons. Our sons, Blaine and Mylan, also couldn't resist the opportunity to comment on my writing.

Dr. Patrick Byrne edited an early version. His revisions tightened and improved the text. Gene Garofalo suggested including additional material. He helped take the book to another level. Dr. John Simon raised some provocative questions. His comments were invaluable. Terry Baxter, Dr. Tom Graves, Roz Liebenthal, Dave Phillips, Myra and Lieutenant Colonel Joe Rakosky, and Lieutenant General Jack Woodmansee provided critical insight and encouragement.

A literary agent's job is to sell your book to the right publisher. Ed Knappman did that and much more. The people at Prentice Hall, especially Tom Power and Yvette Romero, were wonderful.

Finally, I am grateful to the biographers and historians, particularly Bruce Catton, Lloyd Lewis, William S. McFeely, James M. McPherson and Geoffrey Perret, who brought Ulysses S. Grant to life for me.

CONTENTS

CIGARS

"He smokes almost constantly, and, as I then and have since observed, he has a habit of whittling with a small knife. He cuts a small stick into small chips, making nothing. It is evidently a mere occupation of the fingers, his mind all the while intent upon other things. Among men he is nowise noticeable. There is no glitter or parade about him. To me he seems but an earnest businessman."

—from a description of Grant in June 1864

WHISKEY

"I then began to ask them if they knew what he drank, what brand of whiskey he used, telling them most seriously that I wished they would find out. They conferred with each other and concluded they could not tell what brand he used. I urged them to ascertain and let me know, for if it made fighting generals like Grant I should like to get some of it for distribution"

—ABRAHAM LINCOLN
to a delegation of Congressmen that
urged him to remove Grant becuse he drank too much

WINNING

"Sir, if you ever again presume to speak disrespectfully of General Grant in my presence, either you or I will sever his connection with this university."

—ROBERT E. LEE
to a professor at Washington College
where Lee served as president after the Civil War

"To be effective is the job of the executive . . . . Whether he works in a business or in a hospital, in a government agency or in a labor union, in a university or in the army, the executive is, first of all, expected to get the right things done."

Peter Drucker, The Effective Executive

All the quotations are by Ulysses S. Grant, unless otherwise noted.

PREFACE

Ulysses S. Grant was a perceptive and surprisingly modern manager. A pragmatist who learned from his own and others' successes and failures, he brought new dimensions to strategic planning. He was adept at seizing and exploiting opportunities as they presented themselves, and he boldly shattered paradigms long before the term *paradigm* had made its way into the management jargon.

Grant succeeded where everyone else had failed. No one had been able to defeat Robert E. Lee in Virginia, on his home turf. After three years of civil war and a succession of Union commanders, the positions of the Union Army of the Potomac and Lee's Army of Northern Virginia were virtually the same as they had been at the start of the conflict. In spite of Grant's impressive string of victories in Mississippi and Tennessee, few thought he would be successful against his almost-mythic opponent. Members of Grant's staff were told by Army of Potomac veterans that Grant had yet to meet Bobby Lee.

Grant finally did meet Lee, in a yearlong struggle that ended with Lee's defeat. The images from Appomattox are striking: the tall, dignified, resplendent aristocrat from Virginia's finest family surrendering to the mud-spattered son of a Midwestern tannery owner. This is the stuff of the American dream—the underdog scrambling to the top of the heap.

To understand why Grant won, we need to listen to what the men he worked most closely with had to say about him. Lincoln recognized that Grant not only knew the right things to do but would see to it that they got done: "The great thing about Grant...is his perfect correctness and persistency of purpose." Colonel James Rusling remembered him as a man who could "dare great things, and hold on mightily, and toil terribly." He made certain that his subordinates "knew exactly what he wanted, and why, and when he wanted it."

Grant's subordinates praised his common sense, decisiveness, energy, self-control, and self-confidence. Assistant Secretary of War Charles A. Dana described Grant in these words:

Grant was an uncommon fellow—the most modest, the most disinterested and the most honest man I ever knew, with a temper that nothing could disturb and a judgment that was judicial in its comprehensiveness and wisdom. Not a great man except morally; not an original or brilliant man, but sincere, thoughtful, deep and gifted with courage that never faltered.

Recalling an incident during the Vicksburg campaign, when Grant was personally supervising the movement of troops across a bridge, one officer wrote: "There was no nonsense, no sentiment; only a plain business man of the republic, there for the one single purpose of getting that command across the river in the shortest time possible."

Ulysses S. Grant, that "plain business man," never sought fame or glory, nor did he try to tie his performance to personal reward; instead, he concentrated on contribution and service. He looked upon being given increased responsibility not as increasing his power, but as increasing his ability to get the job done. To the Congressman who introduced the bill that would promote him to lieutenant general, Grant wrote:

I feel under many obligations to you for the interest you have taken in my welfare. But recollect that I have been highly honored already by the government and do not ask or feel that I deserve anything more in the shape of honors or promotion. A success over the enemy is what I crave above everything else, and desire to hold such influence over those under my command as to enable me to use them to the best advantage to secure this end.

It is probably true that, but for the Civil War, Grant would have ended his days working in a leather goods store in Galena, Illinois. But had it not been for World War II, wouldn't Dwight D. Eisenhower have retired from the army as a lieutenant colonel and quietly lived out his life in Abilene, Kansas? Grant wrote that "accident often decides the fate of battle." Both Eisenhower and Grant took advantage of the worst kind of accident—war—to make contributions to society that neither of them otherwise would have had the opportunity to make. In doing so, they each compiled a remarkable record of accomplishment.

In 1861, Grant was a clerk in his father's shop. Three years later, he was the commanding general of the United States Army. He was managing an organization of over one million men, the largest in the world. He was overseeing simultaneous operations on multiple fronts that spanned the continent, and he was succeeding where everyone before him had failed.

The fact that Grant won, even though he was "not an original or brilliant man," is what makes his story so compelling. He was not a natural born leader endowed with superhuman managerial abilities. Instead, he was an everyman, but an everyman who learned to get superior performance from ordinary people, and in so doing became a winning manager.

In the fall of 1884, Grant began writing his autobiography. *The Personal Memoirs of U. S. Grant* is a great literary work. What is not so apparent is that it is also a treasure trove of management wisdom. I have used Grant's memoirs and other writings to illustrate a series of practical lessons in management. These cover more than "how to." They address character traits and basic qualities, core beliefs and fundamental values. They are as much about who to be as what to do.

Each lesson is based on an incident in Grant's life. All but two dozen of them are drawn from his management experiences during the Civil War. They are presented in chronological order, so that we see the war as it unfolds through his eyes. The lessons begin with a young Grant registering at West Point. They end with a dying Grant racing the clock to complete his memoirs. In all, they provide us with a fascinating look into the life of an ordinary man who transformed himself into a truly great manager, and in so doing, left us an invaluable legacy.

SEIZE
OPPORTUNITIES

April 1822 – August 1848

Grant's Ohio boyhood ends with his appointment to West Point. His student days at the Academy are spent reading novels and riding horses. Graduated a second lieutenant, he serves with distinction in the Mexican War. During the battle for Mexico City, he sees an opportunity to mount a cannon in a bell tower and seizes upon it. For this decisive action, Grant receives several favorable commendations.

1. BUREAUCRATS DO THE DUMBEST THINGS

HE MAN WE KNOW AS ULYSSES S. GRANT WAS ACTUALLY named Hiram Ulysses Grant. As a boy he was known as Lyss. Thomas Hamer, the Congressman who appointed Grant to West Point, forgot all about the Hiram. Remembering that Grant's mother's maiden name was Simpson and thinking that was Lyss Grant's middle name, he filled out the application in the name of "Ulysses S. Grant."

When Grant arrived at West Point and discovered that the Academy had him registered under the wrong name, he tried to get the error corrected. He was told that it didn't matter what he or his parents thought his name was, the official government application said his name was "Ulysses S." and that application could not be changed. If Hiram U. Grant wanted to attend West Point, he would have to change his name.

LESSON

Bureaucrats will blindly obey whatever set of rules they are instructed to follow even if this leads them to take completely illogical or patently nonsensical actions. Try to keep them out of your organization. Also, help prevent your people from turning into bureaucrats by regularly reminding them that your organization's rules and regulations are designed to provide guidance to intelligent human beings who use their heads, and are not intended for slavish obedience by automatons.

2. KEEP YOUR CARDS TO YOURSELF

*W*HEN HE WAS A BOY, GRANT'S SCHOOLMATES WOULD make him miserable by repeating the story of the time he cajoled his father into letting him purchase a colt from a Mr. Ralston, who lived a few miles from their village. Mr. Ralston was asking twenty-five dollars, while Grant's father felt that twenty dollars was a fair price for the colt.

I at once mounted a horse and went for the colt. When I got to Mr. Ralston's house, I said to him: "Papa says I may offer you twenty dollars for the colt, but if you won't take that, I am to offer twenty-two and a half, and if you won't take that to give you twenty-five." It would not require a Connecticut man to guess the price finally agreed upon. This story is nearly true. I certainly showed very plainly that I had come for the colt and meant to have him. I could not have been over eight years old at the time.

LESSON

It's alright to want something badly, but you can't bargain effectively, anymore than you can win a poker hand, by laying your cards face up on the table.

3. USE DISCIPLINE PURPOSEFULLY

*L*IKE MOST BOYS, GRANT DID NOT LIKE TO WORK. WHILE HE did not recall ever being punished at home, he could not say the same for school.

The rod was freely used there, and I was not exempt from its influence. I can see John D. White—the school teacher—now, with his long beech switch always in his hand. It was not always the same one either. Switches were brought in bundles, from a beech wood near the school house, by the boys for whose benefit they were intended. Often a whole bundle would be used up in a single day. I never had any hard feelings against my teacher, either while attending the school, or in later years when reflecting upon my experience. Mr. White was a kind-hearted man, and was much respected by the community in which he lived.

LESSON

You can maintain the respect of your staff so long as they recognize that your application of discipline is consistent and evenhanded and that you purposefully use discipline to achieve a worthwhile end, not simply because you're heartless.

4. DON'T MISTAKE APPEARANCE FOR ACHIEVEMENT

GRANT ENTERED WEST POINT IN MAY 1839. DURING Grant's freshman year, General Winfield Scott visited the Academy and reviewed the cadets. His appearance made quite an impression upon Grant. "With his commanding figure, his quite colossal size and showy uniform, I thought him the finest specimen of manhood my eyes had ever beheld, and the most to be envied."

Upon graduating, Grant couldn't wait to wear his new uniform. He imagined that his old friends would look upon him with the same mixture of awe and envy that he had felt when he saw General Scott. "I was impatient to get on my uniform and see how it looked, and probably wanted my old school-mates, particularly the girls, to see me in it."

Opposite our house in Bethel stood the old stage tavern where "man and beast" found accommodation. The stable-man was rather dissipated, but possessed of some humor. On my return I found him parading the streets, and attending in the stable, barefooted, but in a pair of sky-blue nankeen pantaloons—just the color of my uniform trousers—with a strip of white cotton sheeting sewed down the outside seams in imitation of mine. The joke was a huge one in the mind of many of the people, and was much enjoyed by them; but I did not appreciate it so highly.

LESSON

Dress for success if you want to, but don't ever, with yourself or others, mistake appearance for achievement.

5. BUT CAN THEY THINK FOR THEMSELVES?

*G*RANT FOUND THE ACADEMIC CURRICULUM AT WEST POINT "very wearisome and uninteresting." He did enjoy mathematics, which came easily to him, and he learned to draw and paint. Grant also spent a great deal of his time reading, and in his senior year served as president of the cadet literary society.

> *There is a fine library connected with the Academy from which cadets can get books to read in their quarters. I devoted more time to these, than to books relating to the course of studies. Much of the time...was devoted to novels, but not those of a trashy sort.*

LESSON

When hiring college graduates for entry-level management positions, look for candidates with a solid grounding in the liberal arts. You can teach bright young people the technical skills they will need, but you shouldn't have to teach them to read with comprehension, write with clarity, or think for themselves. Nor should you have to teach them to be observant, have a sense of perspective, or be able to reason logically. For those entry-level jobs that do require the completion of a technical course of studies, try hiring candidates whose technical curriculum has been well supplemented with a first-rate liberal arts education.

6. ACADEMIC ACHIEVEMENT IS AN UNRELIABLE INDICATOR

*G*RANT WAS ANYTHING BUT A STELLAR STUDENT. HE graduated twenty-first in a class of thirty-nine.

Persons acquainted with the Academy know that the corps of cadets is divided into four companies for the purpose of military exercises. These companies are officered from the cadets, the superintendent and commandant selecting the officers for their military bearing and qualifications.

Grant did make cadet sergeant, but he had so many demerits that he was demoted and served his senior year as a private.

LESSON

Academic achievement, or the lack thereof, is by itself an unreliable indicator of future accomplishment. When interviewing for entry-level management positions, you need to look beyond grades and test scores. It is more important to hire individuals who are intelligent and eager to learn your business, and who can be expected to exercise good judgment and work well with others, than it is to hire academic superstars.

7. ON CLAIMING CREDIT

*A*FTER GRADUATING IN JUNE 1843, GRANT WAS commissioned a second lieutenant and assigned to an infantry regiment. In March 1846, Grant's regiment was ordered to the Rio Grande. War with Mexico broke out in May, and in one of the early engagements, the battle of Resaca de la Palma (May 9, 1846), Grant, in command of a company, led a charge.

There was no resistance, and we captured a Mexican colonel, who had been wounded, and a few men. Just as I was sending them to the rear...a private came from...in advance of where I was. The ground had been charged over before. My exploit was equal to that of the soldier who boasted that he had cut off the leg of one of the enemy. When asked why he did not cut off his head, he replied: "Someone had done that before." This left no doubt in my mind but that the battle of Resaca de la Palma would have been won, just as it was, if I had not been there.

LESSON

Don't kid yourself into believing you made more of a contribution than you actually did, and never claim credit when none is due you. Come down hard on any of your subordinates who try to take more than their fair share of the credit, because if you don't you will be sending the message that you can't differentiate between the deserving and the undeserving, and that will demoralize your entire organization.

8. THE FOLLY OF SWEARING

*I*N AUGUST, GRANT WAS ASSIGNED TO ACT AS QUARTERMASTER for his regiment. Pack mules were hired to transport the army's supplies through the mountainous terrain to Monterrey. Grant was in charge of the pack train and found that managing mules was challenging.

Sometimes one would start to run, bowing his back and kicking up until he scattered his load; others would lie down and try to disarrange their loads by attempting to get on top of them by rolling on them; others with tent-poles for part of their loads would manage to run a tent-pole on one side of a sapling while they would take the other. I am not aware of ever having used a profane expletive in my life; but I would have the charity to excuse those who may have done so, if they were in charge of a train of Mexican pack mules at the time.

When asked why he never cursed, Grant replied:

I never learned to swear. When a boy I seemed to have an aversion to it, and when I became a man I saw the folly of it. I have always noticed, too, that swearing helps to rouse a man's anger; and when a man flies into a passion his adversary who keeps cool always gets the better of him. In fact, I could never see the use of swearing. I think it is the case with many people who swear excessively that it is a mere habit, and that they do not mean to be profane; but, to say the least, it is a great waste of time.

LESSON

There really is no excuse for having a foul mouth. Even if you only occasionally resort to profanity, you still will almost certainly make some of the men and women around you uncomfortable. This in turn will cost you their respect and reduce your effectiveness. If you curse for effect, stop it; it's counterproductive. On the other hand, if you curse because you can't control your temper, then you shouldn't be a manager.

9. WHEN ASSIGNED A SUPPORTING ROLE

*A*S REGIMENTAL QUARTERMASTER AT THE TIME OF THE battle of Monterrey, Grant's orders were to remain in camp and protect his regiment's supplies and other property.

My curiosity got the better of my judgment, and I mounted a horse and rode to the front to see what was going on. I had been there but a short time when an order to charge was given, and lacking the moral courage to return to camp—where I had been ordered to stay—I charged with the regiment.

LESSON

It's natural for you to always want to be where the action is, but if you are assigned a supporting role, carry it out to the best of your ability. Butting in and drawing attention to yourself will not only keep you from doing your job, it will divert others from doing theirs.

10. CREATE A THINKING MACHINE

*W*ATCHING THE SURRENDER OF THE MEXICAN GARRISON AT Monterrey (September 24, 1846), a young Lieutenant Grant was struck by "how little interest the men before me had in the results of the war, and how little knowledge they had of 'what it was all about.'" Years later, General Grant would describe the Union army that marched through Georgia as having been made up of "as good soldiers as ever trod the earth...because they not only worked like a machine but the machine thought."

Our armies were composed of men who were able to read, men who knew what they were fighting for...and so necessarily must have been more than equal to men who fought merely because they were brave and because they were thoroughly drilled and inured to hardships.

LESSON

Empowerment begins with knowledge, which goes beyond job training. No matter how well you teach your people to do their jobs, if they don't understand the organization's mission and the important role they play in carrying it out, all you will have is people who act like non-thinking robots, and you will always be outperformed by any competitors who empower their staff to think for themselves.

11. NOT EVERY PROJECT IS TOP PRIORITY

*I*N JANUARY 1847, GRANT'S REGIMENT WAS PLACED UNDER the command of General William Worth, whose division had been ordered to march to the mouth of the Rio Grande where it would embark on transports to Vera Cruz.

There was not the least reason for haste on the march, for it was known that it would take weeks to assemble shipping enough at the point of our embarkation to carry the army, but General Worth moved his division with a rapidity that would have been commendable had he been going to the relief of a beleagured garrison.... General Worth on one occasion at least, after having made the full distance intended for the day, and after the troops were in camp and preparing their food, ordered tents struck and made the march that night which had been intended for the next day. Some commanders can move troops so as to get the maximum distance out of them without fatigue, while others can wear them out in a few days without accomplishing so much.

LESSON

Don't try to give every project a top priority. To do so would burn out your people, leaving them without the energy and enthusiasm they will need to tackle the next truly important task to come along.

12. SEIZE OPPORTUNITIES

*W*INFIELD SCOTT'S ARMY OCCUPIED MEXICO CITY ON September 14, 1847. On the day before, during the battle for control of the city, Grant saw an opportunity to mount a cannon in a church belfry, and he acted on it.

The effect of this gun upon the troops about the gate of the city was so marked that General Worth saw it from his position. He was so pleased that he....ordered a captain of voltigeurs [light infantry] to report to me with another howitzer to be placed along with the one already rendering so much service. I could not tell the general that there was not room enough in the steeple for another gun.... I took the captain with me, but did not use his gun.

LESSON

If you see an opportunity, seize it. But recognize that there may be limits to the extent to which you can exploit an opportunity, and you will be ineffective if you try to push beyond those limits.

13. NEW PEOPLE NEED EXPERIENCED MANAGERS

*F*ROM GRANT'S PERSPECTIVE, THE AMERICAN VICTORIES IN Mexico against much larger forces were due in large measure to the inexperience of the Mexican officers, and conversely to the education and experience of the American officers and the training they had given to the men in their commands. As a result, new recruits were quickly assimilated into the army, giving the Americans an invaluable advantage.

The volunteers....were associated with so many disciplined men and professionally educated officers, that when they went into engagements it was with a confidence they would not have felt otherwise. They became soldiers themselves almost at once.

LESSON

Assigning new people to experienced managers with well-trained staff is the best way to assimilate them into your organization rapidly, make them productive as quickly as possible, and reduce short-term turnover to a minimum.

14. DON'T BE A MONDAY MORNING QUARTERBACK

*I*N REFLECTING ON HIS MEXICAN WAR EXPERIENCES, GRANT concluded that the battles of Molino del Ray and Chapultepec, both American victories, need never have been fought because the Mexican defenders could have been outflanked and forced to evacuate their positions.

But my later experience has taught me two lessons: first, that things are seen plainer after the events have occurred; second, that the most confident critics are generally those who know the least about the matter criticized.

LESSON

Study past successes and failures carefully, and learn from them. But avoid criticizing others for failing to take advantage of opportunities that only come to light in the glare of hindsight.

15. LIES TEACH NOTHING

*G*RANT WAS ALWAYS TROUBLED BY WHAT HE SAW AS attempts to rewrite history. He believed it was wrong for the Mexican government to celebrate the battle of Chapultepec as though it had been a victory instead of a defeat, and he particularly disliked post–Civil War writers who took the point of view that the Union forces "were slashed around from Donelson to Vicksburg and to Chattanooga; and in the East from Gettysburg to Appomattox, when the physical rebellion gave out from sheer exhaustion."

I would not have the anniversaries of our victories celebrated, nor those of our defeats made fast days and spent in humiliation and prayer; but I would like to see truthful history written.

LESSON

One of the worst mistakes you can make is to lie about what really happened. The great danger is not so much that others will believe your lies, but that you will believe them, thereby preventing you from learning from your mistakes and leading you to make bigger ones in the future.

16. WHAT MATTERS IS EFFECTIVENESS, NOT STYLE

*G*RANT STUDIED TO BE A MANAGER DURING THE MEXICAN War by learning from the successes and failures of the men under whom he served, especially Generals Winfield Scott and Zachary Taylor.

The contrast between the two was very marked. General Taylor never wore uniform, but dressed himself entirely for comfort. He moved about the field in which he was operating to see through his own eyes the situation. Often he would be without staff officers, and when he was accompanied by them there was no prescribed order in which they followed…. General Scott was the reverse in all these particulars. He always wore all the uniform prescribed or allowed by law when he inspected his lines…. His staff…followed, also in uniform and in prescribed order…. But with their opposite characteristics both were great and successful soldiers; both were true, patriotic and upright in all their dealings. Both were pleasant to serve under—Taylor was pleasant to serve with.

LESSON

There is no single perfect management style that suits all. The best management style for you is the one you feel most comfortable with. Your real focus should be on effectiveness, not style. Modify your style if you can, but only if doing so helps you improve your effectiveness as a manager.

17. IF ASKED TO DO THE IMPOSSIBLE

*W*HILE GRANT WAS A GREAT ADMIRER OF GENERAL SCOTT, his hero was Zachary Taylor.

General Taylor was not an officer to trouble the administration much with his demands, but was inclined to do the best he could with the means given him. He felt his responsibility as going no further. If he had thought he was sent to perform an impossibility with the means given him, he would probably have informed the authorities of his opinion and left them to determine what should be done. If the judgment was against him he would have gone on and done the best he could with the means at hand without parading his grievance before the public.

LESSON

By all means tell your boss if you think you're being asked to do the impossible, but if you're told to give it you're best shot, shut up and do so.

FAILURE

August 1848 – April 1861

Grant marries Julia Dent, but on a junior army officer's pay, he cannot afford to take her and their two children with him when his regiment is ordered to California. This separation leads to drinking problems and his resignation from the army. Grant tries farming and real estate, and fails at both.

18. PLAN FOR YOUR FUTURE

*G*RANT NEVER INTENDED TO PURSUE AN ARMY CAREER. HE wanted to be a college professor. After graduating from West Point, he asked to be assigned as an assistant professor of mathematics at the Academy, and that assignment would likely have been approved but for the onset of the war with Mexico. Later, Grant began to give serious consideration to remaining in the Army. He was certain that Thomas Hamer, the Ohio Congressman who had appointed him to West Point, would see to it that he enjoyed a comfortable career as a staff officer. However, Hamer became ill and died during the Mexican War.

I have always believed that had his life been spared, he would have been President of the United States during the term filled by President Pierce. Had Hamer filled that office his partiality for me was such, there is but little doubt I should have been appointed to one of the staff corps of the army—the Pay Department probably.... Neither of these speculations is unreasonable, and they are mentioned to show how little men control their own destiny.

LESSON

Think about your future. Make plans, but always bear in mind that even under the best of circumstances you will have only limited control over the course of future events. Also, don't ever look to the successes, and certainly not to the failures, of others for your advancement.

19. THE ROLE OF FAMILY AND FRIENDS

*U*LYSSES S. GRANT AND JULIA DENT WERE MARRIED IN 1848. Except for a two-year separation when Grant was stationed on the West Coast, they were rarely apart for more than a few weeks at a time during their thirty-seven year marriage. But even before they were married, Julia had already started to play a major role in the life of her future husband. In 1845, shortly before his regiment was ordered to Texas, Grant wrote to Julia.

You can have but little idea of the influence you have over me Julia, even while so far away. If I feel tempted to do any thing that I think is not right I am sure to think, "Well now if Julia saw me would I do so."

LESSON

Your close friends, your family, and especially your mate can be invaluable in the dual role of moral compass and sounding board.

20. WHEN A BARGAIN IS NOT A BARGAIN

*I*N THE SPRING OF 1852, GRANT'S REGIMENT, WITH HIM AS quartermaster, was ordered to California via Panama. The last twenty-five miles of the trip across the Isthmus had to be made by mule-train.

A contract had been entered into with the steamship company in New York for the transportation of the regiment to California, including the Isthmus transit.... But when we reached Cruces there was not a mule, either for pack or saddle, in the place. The contractor promised that the animals would be on hand in the morning. In the morning he said that they were on the way from some imaginary place, and would arrive in the course of the day. This went on until I saw that he could not procure the animals at all at the price he had promised to furnish them for.... I therefore myself dismissed the contractor and made a new contract with a native, at more than double the original price.

LESSON

A supplier who can't deliver as promised is not worth dealing with at any price. If you make price your only consideration, it will almost certainly cost you more in the end. Contracts with suppliers should include performance standards as well as penalty and exit provisions for failure to meet those standards.

21. LAST YEAR'S GOOD IDEA

*W*HEN GRANT ARRIVED IN CALIFORNIA, PRICES FOR supplies were high, so he and three fellow officers got the bright idea that they could raise a crop of potatoes and sell it for a handsome profit.

Our crop was enormous. Luckily for us the Columbia River...overflowed and killed most of our crop. This saved digging it up, for everybody on the Pacific coast seemed to have come to the conclusion at the same time that agriculture would be profitable. In 1853 more than three-quarters of the potatoes raised were permitted to rot in the ground, or had to be thrown away.

LESSON

Last year's good idea may not be so good this year. If the timing isn't right, you'll have a loser.

22. PEOPLE NEED MEANINGFUL WORK

*W*HEN GRANT'S NAME IS MENTIONED, THE FIRST IMAGE most Americans have is that of a hard-drinking general. This characterization of Grant dates from his last pre–Civil War army post, at Fort Humboldt, California. He had left his wife nearly two years earlier, pregnant and with their two-year-old son. Grant was homesick, but more importantly, because he and his commanding officer did not hit it off, he was given no work to do. On February 2, 1854, he wrote a letter to his wife that began: "You do not know how forsaken I feel here.... I do nothing here but sit in my room and read and occasionally take a short ride on one of the public horses." A month later, he wrote: "I have not been a hundred yards from my door but once in the last two weeks." Grant had requested a transfer, but his request had been denied.

My family...consisted now of a wife and two children. I saw no chance of supporting them on the Pacific coast out of my pay as an army officer. I concluded therefore to resign.

Because he had no meaningful responsibilities, Grant's feelings of loneliness were exacerbated. This, in turn, led to increased drinking and his resignation from the army.

LESSON

Without meaningful work, life stinks. People become demoralized and incapacitated. Some become permanently turned off and lose their future potential. Having a chronically underworked staff is every bit as bad as having one that is overworked.

23. FAILURE

*A*FTER REJOINING HIS FAMILY IN 1854, GRANT TRIED HIS hand at farming and real estate. He didn't like either very much, and he failed at both. He lacked adequate capital to make a go of it as a small farmer, and according to his wife, Julia, he was too softhearted to succeed in the real estate business as a rent collector.

I cannot imagine how my dear husband ever thought of going into such a business, as he never could collect a penny that was owed to him.

In May 1860, Grant moved to Galena, Illinois to take a job in his father's leather goods store.

I was nominally only a clerk supporting myself and family on a stipulated salary. In reality my position was different. My father had never lived in Galena himself, but had established my two brothers there.... When I went there it was my father's intention to give up all connection with the business himself, and to establish his three sons in it.

LESSON

A person need not become a failure just by virtue of having been associated with a couple of failed enterprises. Don't be too quick to give up on people who have one or two failures under their belt, especially if they failed at things they really didn't enjoy doing.

24. PRODUCTION DISRUPTIONS

*A*S 1860 DREW TO A CLOSE, THE UNITED STATES WAS again preparing to go to war, this time with itself. Grant foresaw that a Civil War would result in a blockade of Southern ports, and that, in turn, would result in the South's losing its predominant position as the world's foremost exporter of cotton.

This disturbance will give such an impetus to the production of their staple, cotton, in other parts of the world that they can never recover the control of the market again for that commodity.

LESSON

If for whatever reason you stop production, someone else will fill the void, and you will never be able to fully recover your lost market share.

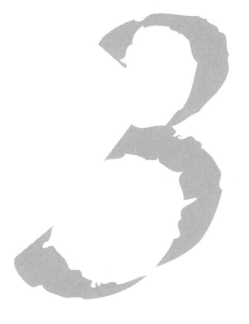

TURN MISTAKES INTO TRAINING OPPORTUNITIES

April – November 1861

The Civil War begins, and Grant, appointed colonel in command of the 21st Illinois regiment, turns an offense punishable by death into a training opportunity. Promoted to brigadier general, he narrowly escapes being taken prisoner.

25. INTERVIEWS REVEAL MORE THAN RESUMES

*A*FTER FORT SUMTER WAS FIRED UPON, GRANT OFFERED his services to the Governor of Illinois and was initially assigned (April 29, 1861) to the Adjutant General's office. About a month later, he went to Cincinnati to pay a call on Major General George McClellan.

I wanted to see him. I had known him slightly at West Point, where we served one year together, and in the Mexican war. I was in hopes that when he saw me he would offer me a position on his staff. I called on two successive days at his office but failed to see him on either occasion.

LESSON

Conducting job interviews is very time-consuming, especially for management positions. But resumes never tell the full story, so try to arrange at least a cursory interview with every candidate who is not obviously unqualified for the vacancy. Otherwise, you could miss a bet by not filling the position with the best person available.

26. A BAD REPUTATION

*S*HORTLY BEFORE ATTEMPTING TO SEE GENERAL McClellan, Grant had written to the Adjutant General of the army requesting that he be appointed to command a regiment.

Having served for fifteen years in the regular army, including four years at West Point, and feeling it the duty of every one who has been educated at the government expense to offer their services for the support of that Government, I have the honor, very respectfully, to tender my services, until the close of the war, in such capacity as may be offered. I would say, in view of my present age and length of service, I feel myself competent to command a regiment.

Grant never received a response to his letter. He was subsequently appointed colonel in command of the 21st Illinois regiment, but by the Governor of Illinois, not the Adjutant General. Perhaps his letter was simply misfiled by some overworked clerk in a harried War Department; or it could be that the story that circulated through the army when Grant resigned (that he had been forced out of the service because of his drinking) was the real reason his letter was misfiled and he did not receive a War Department appointment.

LESSON

A bad reputation is difficult, if not impossible, to shake.

27. WHEN PROMOTED

*G*RANT HAD FELT SOME HESITATION ABOUT BEING APPOINTED a colonel; he was doubtful whether he would be equal to the position.

I had been in all the engagements in Mexico that it was possible for one person to be in; but not in command. If someone else had been colonel and I had been lieutenant-colonel I do not think I would have felt any trepidation.

LESSON

It's not at all uncommon to feel concerned or even frightened when given a promotion. This is especially true for persons going into a management position for the first time, but it also applies to experienced managers who are promoted to a higher level of responsibility. Remember, your boss is confident that you will do a good job; otherwise, you wouldn't be in the position you are. So just take a deep breath and press on.

28. YOU HAVE TO EARN YOUR STRIPES

*U*PON ASSUMING COMMAND OF THE 21ST ILLINOIS INFANTRY regiment, Grant issued the following order (June 18, 1861):

> *In accepting this command, your Commander will require the cooperation of all the commissioned and noncommissioned officers...and hopes to receive also the hearty support of every enlisted man.*

LESSON

When taking on a new management assignment, you can and should insist on receiving the cooperation of the managers who will be reporting to you, but you will have to earn the respect of the rank and file in order to gain their support.

29. PEOPLE NEED STRUCTURE

*G*RANT'S REGIMENT WAS MADE UP OF YOUNG MEN WHO HAD left their homes to go to war. They were a totally undisciplined bunch. Grant's predecessor "had proved to be fully capable of developing all there was in his men of recklessness. It was said that he even went so far at times as to...go with them to the village near by and make a night of it."

I found it very hard work for a few days to bring all the men into anything like subordination; but the great majority favored discipline.

LESSON

No one likes to work in an environment where there are no rules and anything goes. Your people need and want structure, and they will respect you for providing it.

30. TURN MISTAKES INTO TRAINING OPPORTUNITIES

*P*EOPLE'S LIVES ARE AT STAKE ON A BATTLEFIELD, AND mistakes made there are far more costly than any made in an office. In his first week as a regimental commander, some of Grant's men committed an offense so grave that the only punishment provided for under the military law then in effect was execution by a firing squad.

It is with regret that the commanding officer learns that a number of men composing the Guard of last night deserted their posts.... In time of war the punishment of this is death. The Colonel Commanding believing that the men of his command, now in confinement for this offense were ignorant of the magnitude of it, is not disposed to visit them with all the rigor of the law...but would admonish them, and the whole command against a repetition of the offense, as it will not be excused again.

LESSON

Whenever possible, treat errors and mistakes as opportunities for additional training rather than as offenses requiring punishment.

31. FIRST-LINE SUPERVISORS DO THE MOST IMPORTANT TRAINING

*G*RANT RECOGNIZED THAT HIS TOP PRIORITY WAS TO PREPARE his regiment for battle.

Company commanders will have their companies divided into convenient squads and appoint suitable persons to drill them. The officers of Companies are expected to be present and give their personal supervision to these drills, and see that all their men...are present.

LESSON

The critical importance of the first-line supervisor in the training of his or her people cannot be overemphasized. Training courses can teach needed knowledge and skills, but only the first-line supervisor's on-the-job training can weld a group of individuals into a unit that functions effectively.

32. COMMON SENSE

*G*RANT NEEDED TO TEACH HIS REGIMENT THE BATTALION drill, that is, the tactics that he would use for troop movements. But Grant had graduated from West Point at the bottom of his class in tactics, and had not been at a battalion drill since the summer of 1846. In the intervening fifteen years, the army had adopted William Hardee's tactics. Grant got a copy "and studied one lesson, intending to confine the exercise of the first day to the commands I had thus learned."

We were encamped just outside of town on the common, among scattering suburban houses with enclosed gardens, and when I got my regiment in line and rode to the front I soon saw that if I attempted to follow the lesson I had studied I would have to clear away some of the houses and garden fences to make room. I perceived at once, however, that Hardee's tactics...was nothing more than common sense.... I found no trouble in giving commands that would take my regiment where I wanted it to go and carry it around all obstacles. I do not believe that the officers of the regiment ever discovered that I had never studied the tactics that I used.

LESSON

You will rarely, if ever, go wrong by relying on common sense.

33. GO HEAD TO HEAD

*I*N JULY 1861, GRANT'S REGIMENT WAS ORDERED TO MOVE against the camp of Confederate Colonel Thomas Harris. As he approached the camp, Grant's heart was in his throat.

> *The place where Harris had been encamped a few days before was still there...but the troops were gone. My heart resumed its place. It occurred to me at once that Harris had been as much afraid of me as I had been of him. This was a view of the question I had never taken before; but it was one I never forgot afterwards. From that event to the close of the war, I never experienced trepidation upon confronting an enemy, though I always felt more or less anxiety. I never forgot that he had as much reason to fear my forces as I had his. The lesson was valuable.*

LESSON

Never be afraid to go head to head against your competitors. They are likely to be as concerned about you as you are about them.

34. NOBODY IS BETTER THAN A BAD BODY

*I*N EARLY AUGUST, GRANT LEARNED THAT HE HAD BEEN promoted to brigadier general. He was ordered to Ironton, Missouri where Colonel B. Gratz Brown was in command. Confederate General Hardee (the author of the book on tactics) was believed to be just twenty-five miles away.

Colonel Brown's command was very demoralized. A squadron of cavalry could have ridden into the valley and captured the entire force. Brown himself was gladder to see me on that occasion than he ever has been since. I relieved him and sent all his men home, within a day or two, to be mustered out of service.

LESSON

You are always better off to operate shorthanded, with unfilled positions, than you are to retain poor or unreliable performers.

35. STAY IN THE GAME

*I*N LATE AUGUST, BRIGADIER GENERAL BENJAMIN PRENTISS came under the command of Brigadier General Grant. Prentiss was so displeased at having to report to another brigadier general that he requested and received reassignment.

General Prentiss made a great mistake on the above occasion.... In consequence of this occurrence he was off duty in the field when the principal campaign at the West was going on, and his juniors received promotion while he was where none could be obtained.

LESSON

If, because of false pride or perceived slights, you take yourself out of the action and consequently miss opportunities for advancement, you have no one to blame but yourself.

36. FERTILIZE YOUR GARDEN EVENLY

*W*HEN THE CIVIL WAR BEGAN, THE PROFESSIONAL soldiers in the North "were retained, generally with their old commands and rank, until the war had lasted many months. In the [Union] Army of the Potomac there was what was known as the 'regular brigade,' in which, from the commanding officer down to the youngest second lieutenant, every one was educated in his profession." By comparison, newly formed Union units were without experienced soldiers. "Some of these went into battle at the beginning under division commanders who were entirely without military training. This gave me an idea...that the government ought to disband the regular army."

Grant's idea never received serious consideration. His superiors at that time were trapped in the paradigm that the regular army was essential, and they could not envision saving the Union without it. But Grant realized that the great advantage the South had over the North when the war began was that the South had no standing army, and as a result, the South's "trained soldiers had to find employment with the troops from their own States. In this way what there was of military education and training was distributed throughout their whole army. The whole loaf was leavened."

LESSON

The surest recipe for disaster is an inexperienced manager with a staff of new people. Don't hesitate to spread your experienced people throughout your organization. While it is true that to do so will weaken some units, the overall improvement in organizational effectiveness will more than compensate for any short-term deficiencies.

37. PURCHASING

*I*N SEPTEMBER 1861, GRANT ARRIVED IN CAIRO, ILLINOIS where he had been ordered to take command. He discovered that he had inherited a corrupt quartermaster who was in league with a group of contractors who had a virtual monopoly on the business of supplying the army. Grant promptly replaced the quartermaster. When presented with a demand for a voucher for payment on a contract for forage that had been let at a much higher price than the going fair market value, Grant said no.

My reply to them was that they had got their contract without my consent... I would not approve a voucher for them under that contract if they never got a cent. Hoped they would not. This forced them to...sell the forage for what it was worth.

LESSON

Your purchasing process needs to be competitive, open, and honest. Frequent, unscheduled, independent audits will help keep it that way.

38. GIVE NO SPECIAL FAVORS

S A GENERAL, GRANT COULD GIVE JOBS AND LET contracts to friends and relatives. He also could arrange for them to receive special favors. Grant would have none of it.

Regarding the horde of job seekers, Grant wrote to his sister Mary, "I do not want to be importuned for places.... My influence no doubt would secure places with those under me, but I become directly responsible for the suitableness of the appointee.... I always want to be in a condition to do my duty without partiality, favor or affection."

When Grant's father Jesse wanted to sell leather goods to the army, Grant refused to help him: "It is necessary both to my efficiency for the public good and my own reputation that I should keep clear of government contracts."

Julia Grant's brother, John, was a confederate prisoner, but when she asked her husband to arrange a special prisoner exchange for the release of her brother, Grant refused to do so, even though such exchanges were a fairly common practice. According to Julia, John "did not get back until the general exchange of prisoners...at the close of the war."

LESSON

For the good of your organization, family and friends should not receive special treatment.

39. THE COURAGE TO TELL IT LIKE IT IS

*O*NE OF GRANT'S FIRST ACTS UPON BEING PROMOTED TO brigadier general was to name John Rawlins as his adjutant. When rumors about Grant's drinking started circulating, Rawlins wrote to one of Grant's supporters, Congressman Washburne: "I would say unequivocally and emphatically that the statement that General Grant is drinking very hard is utterly untrue and could have originated only in malice." Rawlins would rush to Grant's defense if he had been falsely accused, but when in June 1863, during a lull in the Vicksburg campaign, Rawlins became concerned that Grant may have started drinking again, he lost no time taking Grant to task in a sharply worded letter.

The great solicitude I feel for the safety of this army leads me to mention what I had hoped never again to do—the subject of your drinking. This may surprise you, for I may be (and trust I am) doing you an injustice by unfounded suspicions, but if an error it better be on the side of this country's safety than in fear of offending a friend. I have heard that Dr. McMillan, at General Sherman's a few days ago, induced you, notwithstanding your pledge to me, to take a glass of wine.... If my suspicions are unfounded, let my friendship for you and my zeal for my country be my excuse for this letter; and if they are correctly founded, and you determine not to heed the admonitions and the prayers of this hasty note by immediately ceasing to touch a single drop of any kind of liquor, no matter by whom asked or under what circumstances, let my immediate relief from duty in this department be the result.

LESSON

Surround yourself with men and women of unquestioned integrity, who have the courage to tell you when they think what you're doing is wrong. Don't be one of those managers who cut off criticism by saying that they don't like what they're hearing. You may not like it, and you may not agree with it, but you will be better off for having heard it.

40. KNOW WHEN TO KEEP YOUR MOUTH SHUT

*G*RANT LEARNED AN INVALUABLE LESSON EARLY IN THE WAR when, as a result of a prisoner exchange, he received orders to allow freed Confederates to pass through his lines. Grant had known a number of these men before the war.

Such of them as I had known were received at my headquarters [in Cairo] as old acquaintances, and ordinary routine business was not disturbed by their presence. On one occasion when several were present in my office my intention to visit Cape Girardeau [Missouri] the next day, to inspect the troops at that point, was mentioned. Something transpired which postponed my trip; but a steamer employed by the government was passing...the next day, when a section of rebel artillery with proper escort brought her to. A major, one of those who had been at my headquarters the day before, came at once aboard and after some search made a direct demand for my delivery.

LESSON

Be closemouthed. There is never a good reason for telling competitors and third parties more than they need to know. Also, be especially careful when talking to old friends who find themselves in changed circumstances with new loyalties.

KNOW
YOUR COMPETITION

November 1861 – April 1862

The battle of Belmont, his first Civil War action, gives Grant confidence. He uses his personal knowledge of the Confederate commander at Fort Donelson to his advantage and captures the 12,000-man garrison defending the fort. Grant's capture of Fort Donelson gives the Union its first major victory and earns him promotion to major general. The press begins referring to him as Unconditional Surrender Grant.

41. IT AIN'T OVER 'TIL...

*O*N NOVEMBER 7, 1861, GRANT LED TROOPS IN BATTLE for the first time in the Civil War when he attacked a Confederate encampment at Belmont, Missouri. After four hours of fierce fighting, his forces entered the Confederate camp.

The moment the camp was reached our men laid down their arms and commenced rummaging the tents to pick up trophies. Some of the higher officers were little better than the privates. They galloped about from one cluster of men to another and at every halt delivered a short eulogy upon the Union cause and the achievements of the command. All this time the men we had been engaged with for four hours, lay crouched under cover of the river bank, ready to come up and surrender if summoned to do so, but finding they were not pursued, they worked their way up the river and came up on the bank between us and our transports.

LESSON

Avoid premature celebrations. They'll lull you into a false sense of security. Manage important projects as if you were running downhill in front of an avalanche; you can't afford to stop halfway down the hill, look back, and reflect upon how well you've done so far. Also, don't congratulate others "until bottom has been struck."

42. BE WILLING TO PULL THE PLUG

*A*T BELMONT, THE UNION CELEBRATION WAS SHORT-LIVED.

The men we had driven over the bank were seen in line up the river between us and our transports. The alarm "surrounded" was given.... At first some of the officers seemed to think that to be surrounded was to be placed in a hopeless position, where there was nothing to do but surrender. But when I announced that we had cut our way in and could cut our way out just as well, it seemed a new revelation to officers and soldiers.

Later in the war, when Sherman's army was marching through Georgia, Lincoln sought assurances from Grant that Sherman would not be cut off and surrounded.

I heard afterwards of Mr. Lincoln's saying to those who would inquire of him as to what he thought about the safety of Sherman's army, that Sherman was alright: "Grant says they are safe with such a general, and if they cannot get out where they want to, they can crawl back by the hole they went in at."

LESSON

You will usually be able to extricate yourself from even the worst messes if you are willing to back out, but not if you insist on stubbornly pushing forward. Organizations that try to implement a poorly designed or tested system, and stick with it because they lack the courage to admit that the implementation was premature, can dig themselves into so deep a hole that when they finally do admit their mistake, the cost of backing out is enormous.

43. KNOW YOUR COMPETITION

*G*RANT BELIEVED ONE OF THE GREAT ADVANTAGES HE derived from his years at West Point and his Mexican War experience was having been brought into personal contact with many of the men he would both serve with and oppose during the Civil War.

The acquaintance thus formed was of immense service to me in the war of the rebellion—I mean what I learned of the characters of those to whom I was afterwards opposed. I do not pretend to say that all movements, or even many of them, were made with special reference to the characteristics of the commander against whom they were directed. But my appreciation of my enemies was certainly affected by this knowledge.

In February 1862, Grant captured Fort Donelson, Tennessee, giving the Union its first major victory. Grant chose to move against a larger and entrenched enemy force without waiting for reinforcements because he had known the Confederate commander, General Gideon Pillow, in Mexico, "and judged that with any force, no matter how small, I could march up to within gunshot of any entrenchments he was given to hold."

After Fort Donelson surrendered, Grant had a friendly conversation with his old friend, Confederate General Simon Buckner: "He said to me that if he had been in command I would not have got up to Donelson as easily as I did. I told him that if he had been in command I should not have tried in the way I did."

LESSON

Study your competition. If at all possible, get to know them personally. The most valuable lessons of all are those learned from and about your competitors.

44. CONFRONTING DISASTER

*T*HE DAY BEFORE THE CONFEDERATES AT FORT DONELSON surrendered, they attacked in a desperate attempt to break through Grant's lines. Grant, who was away at the time of the attack, was informed that some of his forces were scattered and in full retreat. He hurried to the scene of the disaster.

> *I saw the men standing in knots talking in the most excited manner. No officer seemed to be giving any directions.... I directed Colonel [Joseph] Webster to ride with me and call out to the men as we passed: "Fill your cartridge-boxes, quick, and get into line; the enemy is trying to escape and he must not be permitted to do so." This acted like a charm. The men only wanted someone to give them a command.*

LESSON

When confronted with a disaster, size up the situation as quickly as possible, determine what needs to be done, then let all those affected know what you think the problem is and what you intend to do about it. Above all, remain calm. Calmness in the face of disaster inspires confidence.

45. PROVIDE THE TOOLS

*O*NE REASON FOR THE INITIAL SUCCESS OF THE Confederate attack was that General John McClernand's division had run out of ammunition.

His men had stood up gallantly until the ammunition in their cartridge-boxes ran out. There was abundance of ammunition near by lying on the ground in boxes, but at that stage of the war it was not all of our commanders of regiments, brigades, or even divisions, who had been educated up to the point of seeing that their men were constantly supplied with ammunition during an engagement.

LESSON

You can't expect your people to get the job done if you don't see to it that they have the tools they need to do it.

46. GIFT HORSES

*G*RANT IS ALWAYS PICTURED WITH A LIGHTED CIGAR, BUT prior to the capture of Fort Donelson, he had been primarily a pipe smoker. The morning the Confederates attacked his troops surrounding the fort, Grant was visiting with Flag-Officer Foote, who had offered Grant a cigar. Upon leaving the flagship to return to his headquarters, Grant had no sooner lit his cigar when he learned of the Confederate attack.

I galloped forward at once, and while riding among the troops giving directions for repulsing the assault I carried the cigar in my hand.... In the accounts published in the papers I was represented as smoking a cigar in the midst of the conflict; and many persons...sent me boxes of the choicest brands.... As many as ten thousand were soon received. I gave away all I could get rid of, but having such a quantity on hand, I naturally smoked more than I would have done under ordinary circumstances.

Grant died of throat cancer at the age of sixty-three.

LESSON

Know when to look a gift horse in the mouth.

47. IT'S NOT IMPORTANT WHO GETS THE CREDIT

*D*URING THE FORT DONELSON CAMPAIGN, GENERAL William T. Sherman, whose forces were at the mouth of the Cumberland River, was ordered to send reinforcements and supplies to Grant. The manner in which he did so forever secured him a place in Grant's heart.

At that time he was my senior in rank and there was no authority of law to assign a junior to command a senior of the same grade. But every boat that came up with supplies or reinforcements brought a note of encouragement from Sherman, asking me to call upon him for any assistance he could render and saying that if he could be of service at the front I might send for him and he would waive rank.

LESSON

Don't ever let position or chain of command prevent you from doing your job, especially when your job involves helping others do theirs. A great deal can be accomplished if you don't worry about who is going to get the credit.

48. SEE FOR YOURSELF WHAT'S HAPPENING

*G*RANT ALWAYS TRIED TO BE ACCESSIBLE TO THE TROOPS under his command. He would circulate among them, chat and kid with them. While talking with a wounded soldier who was bragging about how effective his musket fire had been, Grant jokingly asked:

You didn't hurt anyone, did you?

Why, General, I dunno—I reckon I just scared them and they fainted.

LESSON

It's important for managers at every level in the organization to walk through the work areas and talk with the people on the job. It's a way for you to see for yourself what's happening. If you have the knack for it, lighthearted, inoffensive humor can be used effectively as an icebreaker and morale builder. On the other hand, offensive or tasteless jokes will have the opposite effect.

49. PROJECT DELAYS ARE COSTLY

$\mathcal{G}$RANT WAS DISAPPOINTED THAT AFTER HIS CAPTURE OF
Fort Donelson, he was not permitted to move quickly to extend
the territory under Union control to encompass all of Tennessee
and Mississippi. As he explained in a letter to his wife:

> *I want to push on as rapidly as possible to save hard fighting.
> These terrible battles are very good things to read about for persons who
> lose no friends but I am decidedly in favor of having as little of it as pos-
> sible. The way to avoid it is to push forward as vigorously as possible.*

LESSON

Delays resulting from a lack of vigor in managing a project are
always costly.

50. TWO COMMANDERS ARE ONE TOO MANY

*G*RANT BELIEVED THAT IF THE VICTORY AT DONELSON HAD been promptly followed by a drive south the Union forces would have encountered little resistance.

If one general who would have taken the responsibility had been in command of all of the troops west of the Alleghenies, he could have marched to Chattanooga, Corinth, Memphis and Vicksburg with the troops we then had.

At this time General Albert Sidney Johnston commanded all the Confederate troops west of the Allegheny Mountains, with the exception of those in the extreme south. On the National side the forces confronting him were divided into, at first three, then four separate departments. Johnston had greatly the advantage in having supreme command over all troops that could possibly be brought to bear upon one point, while the forces similarly situated on the National side, divided into independent commands, could not be brought into harmonious action except by orders from Washington.

LESSON

The best way to insure that a project will be successfully completed is to assign a single project leader with full authority to take whatever actions are necessary, including giving directions to persons that don't ordinarily report to the project leader. Never forget that "two commanders on the same field are always one too many."

51. TALK TO YOUR BOSS

*L*ESS THAN THREE WEEKS AFTER CAPTURING FORT
Donelson, for which he had been promoted to major general,
Grant's performance was being seriously questioned and his posi-
tion was in jeopardy. This followed a period of time during which
Grant had been out of communication with his superior, General
Henry W. Halleck.

*Later I learned that General Halleck had been calling lustily for
more troops.... McClellan asked him what force he had. Halleck
telegraphed me to supply the information so far as my command was
concerned, but I received none of his dispatches. At last Halleck reported
to Washington that he had repeatedly ordered me to give the strength of
my force, but could get nothing out of me; that I had gone to Nashville,
beyond the limits of my command, without his authority, and that my
army was more demoralized by victory than the army at Bull Run had
been by defeat. General McClellan, on this information, ordered that I
should be relieved from duty.*

LESSON

Talk to your boss. If you aren't frequently communicating with the
person you are reporting to, you're asking for trouble. Your boss
will begin to have doubts and start imagining things. Others, jealous of your success (unfortunately there are always a few in any
organization), will feed your boss' fears with unsubstantiated
rumors. For you it will be a nightmare, one that could easily have
been prevented, if only you had remembered to make communicating with the person you report to one of your top priorities.

52. IF FALSELY ACCUSED

On March 4, 1861, General Halleck sent Grant a telegram in which he accused him of disobedience for failing to report the strength of his command. The following day, Grant replied:

I am not aware of ever having disobeyed any order from head-quarters—certainly never intended such a thing. I have reported almost daily the condition of my command.... In conclusion I will say that you may rely on my carrying out your instructions in every particular to the very best of my ability.

LESSON

If you are falsely accused of wrongdoing, unemotionally set the record straight, and try to do so in such a manner as to allow you to resume amicable relations with the person who attacked you.

53. ON REPORTING TO A FORMER SUBORDINATE

*G*RANT BELIEVED THAT THE UNDERLYING REASON FOR General Halleck's attempt to have him relieved of command was because Halleck wanted to replace Grant with General Charles F. Smith.

> *It is probable that the general opinion was that Smith's long services in the army and distinguished deeds rendered him the more proper person for such command. Indeed I was rather inclined to this opinion myself at that time, and would have served as faithfully under Smith as he had done under me.*

Later in the war, upon being placed in command of all the Union armies, Grant recommended that General Don Carlos Buell be restored to duty. Buell declined:

> *...saying that it would be degradation to accept the assignment offered. I understood afterwards that he refused to serve under either Sherman or [E. R. S.] Canby because he had ranked them both.... The worst excuse a soldier can make for declining service is that he once ranked the commander he is ordered to report to.*

LESSON

You will have the opportunity to work with people both more and less capable than yourself. If you are lucky, you will have the privilege of having people work for you who are more capable than you. At some point, you may find yourself reporting to someone who was formerly your subordinate. If that occurs, don't go sit in your tent and sulk. When that person was working for you, he or she undoubtedly turned in a stellar performance that inured to your credit. Now you owe no less.

SEE
THE TOTAL PICTURE

April 6 – 7, 1862

Nearly one man in four is killed, wounded, or captured, over twenty thousand in all, on the bloody battlefield at Shiloh. At the end of the first day's fighting, even Sherman believes that the Union army must retreat. Grant, who has been to every point on the field and can see the total picture, knows better. The next day he orders a counterattack. The Confederates retreat, and Grant wins one of the costliest battles of the war.

54. RETAIN YOUR HUMANITY

*B*EFORE LEAVING MEXICO IN 1848, GRANT HAD ATTENDED a bullfight, "not wishing to leave the country without having witnessed the national sport. The sight to me was sickening. I could not see how human beings could enjoy the sufferings of beasts, and often of men, as they seemed to do on these occasions."

Grant commanded the Union forces at the battle of Shiloh (Tennessee), which was fought on the 6th and 7th of April 1862. At the end of the first day's fighting, Grant's army had been forced back, and the Confederates occupied the tents that the Union troops had slept in the previous night. Grant and his men had to sleep in the open. Grant, who was in great pain from a badly swollen ankle (a consequence of his horse having fallen on him three days earlier), made his headquarters under a tree. Rain began to fall in torrents.

I moved to the log-house under the bank. This had been taken as a hospital, and all night wounded men were being brought in, their wounds dressed, a leg or an arm amputated as the case might require, and everything being done to save life or alleviate suffering. The sight was more unendurable than encountering the enemy's fire, and I returned to my tree in the rain.

LESSON

Don't be callous or indifferent to the sufferings of others, especially if their suffering results from actions that you felt compelled to take. You can't let the fact that some or even many will suffer stop you from doing what's necessary for the good of the organization, but you can make certain that what you have to do is done as humanely as possible.

55. TEACH THE MOST IMPORTANT LESSONS FIRST

*G*RANT WAS CRITICIZED FOR NOT HAVING THE FORESIGHT TO have his troops dug in and behind fortifications at Shiloh.

The troops with me, officers and men, needed discipline and drill more than they did experience with the pick, shovel and axe. Reinforcements were arriving almost daily, composed of troops that had been hastily thrown together into companies and regiments—fragments of incomplete organizations, the men and officers strangers to each other. Under all these circumstances I concluded that drill and discipline were worth more to our men than fortifications.

LESSON

Having a well-trained staff is critically important. However, since you can't teach new people everything they need to know all at once, be sure you teach the most important lessons first. Usually, those are the ones that allow them to begin to contribute to the organization in the shortest possible time frame.

56. THE ILLUSION OF COMMUNICATION

*A*T THE START OF THE BATTLE, GRANT SENT ONE OF HIS staff officers to General Lew Wallace, whose division was some miles away, with orders for him to immediately march to the battlefield "by the road nearest the river." Wallace took a different route, and as a result, arrived too late to participate in the first day of the battle. The presence of his division on the field that day would have made an enormous difference.

My order was to follow the road nearest the river. But my order was verbal, and to a staff officer who was to deliver it to General Wallace, so that I am not competent to say just what order the General actually received.

LESSON

Important instructions need to be delivered face-to-face or in writing. They should never be delivered verbally through a third party; that is a surefire recipe for creating the most common of all communication problems—the illusion that the message has been correctly transmitted and understood.

57. FREQUENT MANAGEMENT CHANGES

*A*T THE TIME OF THE BATTLE, GENERAL CHARLES F. SMITH was too ill to take the field. His division was commanded by Brigadier General W. H. L. Wallace.

Wallace was mortally wounded in the first day's engagement, and with the change of commanders thus necessarily effected in the heat of battle the efficiency of his division was much weakened. [At the end of that day,] the division...as much from the disorder arising from changes of division and brigade commanders, under heavy fire, as from any other cause, had lost its organization and did not occupy a place in the line.

LESSON

Frequent management changes demoralize an organization, particularly if they occur at times when the going is rough. They should be avoided if at all possible. If unavoidable, they should be planned as carefully as circumstances permit to minimize the discomfort of the staff and the consequent disruption of their work.

58. EQUALS AND UNEQUALS

*D*URING THAT FIRST DAY AT SHILOH, GRANT "WAS continuously engaged in passing from one part of the field to another, giving directions to division commanders."

In thus moving along the line, however, I never deemed it important to stay long with Sherman. Although his troops were then under fire for the first time, their commander by his constant presence with them, inspired a confidence in officers and men that enabled them to render services on that bloody battle-field worthy of the best of veterans.

LESSON

Not all of your subordinates require equal attention. You need to spend some time, but not the same amount of time, with each of them. Give the bulk of your time and attention to those who need it the most. You do your organization a disservice when you give equal treatment to those who are unequal.

59. WHERE YOU STAND AFFECTS WHAT YOU SEE

*M*ORE THAN HALF OF GRANT'S ARMY THAT FIRST DAY had never before been in battle. Many of these men broke and ran when the Confederates attacked. Later that day, General Buell (who was bringing up reinforcements) arrived, and he and Grant met in the rear of the Union lines.

At that time there probably were as many as four or five thousand stragglers lying under cover of the river bluff, panic-stricken, most of whom would have been shot where they lay, without resistance, before they would have taken muskets and marched to the front to protect themselves.... I have no doubt that this sight impressed General Buell with the idea that a line of retreat would be a good thing just then. If he had come in by the front instead of through the stragglers in the rear, he would have thought and felt differently. Could he have come through the Confederate rear, he would have witnessed there a scene similar to that at our own. The distant rear of an army engaged in battle is not the best place from which to judge correctly what is going on in front.

LESSON

Don't judge or be critical of others if you are not close enough to what they are doing to know what is really happening. Where you stand affects what you see.

60. SEE THE TOTAL PICTURE

*S*HERMAN ALSO BELIEVED THAT THE UNION ARMY SHOULD retreat. Grant, however, having been to every part of the battle-field, consulting with his commanders and seeing for himself, had a different perspective. When asked if he was planning to retreat, Grant replied:

Oh no. They can't break our lines tonight—it is too late. Tomorrow we shall attack...and drive them, of course.

LESSON

You need to see the total picture before you can make realistic assessments.

61. PUSH YOUR INHERENT ADVANTAGES

*A*T SHILOH, THE TENNESSEE RIVER RAN BEHIND THE Union lines, and the river was controlled by Union gunboats. Toward the end of the first day of the battle, naval gunfire helped repel a Confederate attempt to turn Grant's left flank.

After nightfall, when firing had entirely ceased on land, the commander of the fleet...suggested the idea of dropping a shell within the lines of the enemy every fifteen minutes during the night. This was done with effect, as is proved by the Confederate reports.

LESSON

If you have an inherent advantage over your competition, push it to the max.

62. COMMITTEES STUDY GOOD IDEAS TO DEATH

$\mathcal{G}$ENERAL ALBERT SIDNEY JOHNSTON COMMANDED THE Confederate forces at the battle of Shiloh. While Johnston showed great personal courage, he was, in Grant's judgement, "vacillating and undecided in his actions."

We have the authority of his son and biographer for saying that his plan was to attack the forces at Shiloh and crush them; then to cross the Tennessee [River] and destroy the army of Buell, and push the war across the Ohio River. The design was a bold one; but we have the same authority for saying that in the execution Johnston showed vacillation and indecision. He left Corinth on the 2nd of April and was not ready to attack until the 6th. The distance his army had to march was less than twenty miles. Johnston...held a council of war...on the morning of the fifth. On the evening of the same day he was in consultation with some of his generals...and still again on the morning of the 6th. During this last consultation, and before a decision had been reached, the battle began by the National troops opening fire on the enemy.

LESSON

The best way to kill a good idea is to submit it to a committee to study.

63. SUCCEEDING A POPULAR MANAGER

ALBERT SIDNEY JOHNSTON WAS A VERY POPULAR AND highly regarded general. There are some writers who believe that had he not been mortally wounded during the first day's fighting, the Confederates would have won a decisive victory.

General [P. G. T.] Beauregard was next in rank to Johnston and succeeded to the command, which he retained to the close of the battle.... His tactics have been severely criticized by Confederate writers, but I do not believe his fallen chief could have done any better under the circumstances.

LESSON

It's always tough to succeed a popular manager, and especially so under adverse conditions. If you promote a subordinate into such a position, don't make the mistake of expecting your newly promoted manager to be a carbon copy of his or her predecessor, and don't fall into the trap of second-guessing his or her every move. Doing so will only make it harder for the person to be successful. Give the new manager a chance to put his or her own spin on the job.

64. BE STEADFAST

*I*N COMMENTING ON THE BATTLE, GRANT WROTE:

Shiloh was the severest battle fought at the West during the war, and but few in the East equalled it for hard, determined fighting.... The result was a Union victory that gave the men who achieved it great confidence in themselves ever after....

The Confederates fought with courage at Shiloh.... It is possible that the Southern man started in with a little more dash than his Northern brother; but he was correspondingly less enduring.

LESSON

In the final analysis, how well you start a project doesn't matter; how you finish it does. Steadfastness is required to see great endeavors carried through to successful conclusions.

65. TRUST, BUT VERIFY

*T*HE CASUALTY LISTS FROM THE BATTLE OF SHILOH CAUSED such revulsion in the North that there were cries for Grant's removal. Lincoln responded, "I can't spare this man: he fights." Lincoln was going to stick with Grant, but he wasn't going to do it blindly. He had Secretary of War Stanton send a telegram to Grant's superior, General Halleck.

> *The President desires to know.... whether any neglect or misconduct of General Grant or any other officer contributed to the sad casualties that befell our forces.*

Halleck, who was no fan of Grant's, could find nothing to criticize about the conduct of the battle.

LESSON

You need to stick with your top performers, even if they occasionally deliver results that are not to your liking. While they are entitled to your support, that support cannot be given blindly. When you have a legitimate cause for concern, take the time to investigate.

66. CORRECT ALL MISSTATEMENTS

*I*N THE SUMMER OF 1884, GRANT WROTE A MAGAZINE ARTICLE about the battle of Shiloh. In that article, he criticized General Alexander McCook for his reluctance to pursue the retreating Confederates on the second day of the battle. On further reflection, Grant decided that McCook had been correct in believing that his troops were in no condition to go after their fleeing foe.

I did General McCook injustice in my article.... I am not willing to do anyone an injustice, and if convinced that I have done one, I am always willing to make the fullest admission.

LESSON

All misstatements, especially negative comments about someone's performance, need to be corrected immediately.

DON'T SCATTER
YOUR RESOURCES

April 1862 – January 1863

General Halleck, Grant's superior, assumes personal command of the army and takes two months to advance the twenty miles from Shiloh to Corinth, Mississippi. After occupying Corinth, Halleck disperses his forces. As a result, Grant, who replaces him as department commander, is forced on the defensive.

67. RESPECT THE CHAIN OF COMMAND

*O*N APRIL 11, 1862, GENERAL HALLECK ARRIVED AT Grant's headquarters and took command of the army. Grant was second in command, and also had nominal command of the right wing and the reserve.

Orders were sent direct [by Halleck] to the right wing or reserve, ignoring me, and advances were made from one line of entrenchments to another without notifying me.

When Grant became commanding general of all the Union armies, he quickly came to the conclusion that he could be most effective if he made his headquarters in the field with General George Meade's Army of the Potomac. But he resolved not to do to Meade what Halleck had done to him.

I tried to make General Meade's position as nearly as possible what it would have been if I had been in Washington or any other place away from his command. I therefore gave all movements for the Army of the Potomac to Meade to have them executed. To avoid the necessity of having to give orders direct, I established my headquarters near his, unless there were reasons for locating them elsewhere. This sometimes happened, and I had on occasions to give orders direct to the troops affected.

LESSON

When giving direction, it is generally a bad idea to skip over the chain of command. Feel free to gather information from anyone in the organization, but don't tell someone who works for one of your subordinates what to do unless immediate action is required. If you make a practice of going around the people who report to you, you will undermine their authority and show that you lack confidence in their abilities, thereby making it impossible for them to do their jobs.

68. WRITE PERSONAL NOTES

*W*HEN, ON APRIL 25TH, GENERAL CHARLES F. SMITH DIED from an infected leg injury, Grant wrote to his wife.

> *It was my fortune to have gone through West Point with the general and to have served with him in all his battles in Mexico and in this rebellion, and I can bear honest testimony to his great worth as a soldier and a friend. Where an entire nation condoles with you in your bereavement no one can do so with more heartfelt grief than myself.*

LESSON

There is no excuse for not writing a personal note whether it be of condolence or congratulations. Greeting cards are used by lazy modern-day managers who neither know nor care about their people.

69. KNOW WHEN TO HEED YOUR SUBORDINATES

*G*ENERAL HALLECK BEGAN A SLOW, PONDEROUS MOVEMENT against Corinth, Mississippi, twenty miles away. During the advance, Grant made a suggestion to him regarding the army's route of march. "I was silenced so quickly that I felt that possibly I had suggested an unmilitary movement."

Four months later, in September 1862, while making preparations to attack Confederate General Sterling Price's forces at Iuka, Mississippi, General William Rosecrans made a suggestion, and Grant (unlike Halleck) listened to his subordinate.

General Rosecrans had previously had his headquarters at Iuka.... While there he had a most excellent map prepared showing all the roads and streams in the surrounding country. He was also personally familiar with the ground, so that I deferred very much to him in my plans.

LESSON

Don't ever reject a subordinate's suggestions out of hand, and always make an extra effort to be open-minded when your subordinate is closer to the details than you are.

70. INSUFFERABLE BOSSES

*A*FTER THE CONFEDERATES EVACUATED CORINTH AND THE Union forces occupied the town (May 30, 1862), General Halleck continued to give orders directly to Grant's subordinates. He so totally ignored Grant that Grant found himself in the embarrassing and, to him, unendurable position of being a commander "with a nominal command and yet no command."

I had repeatedly asked...to be relieved from duty under Halleck; but all my applications were refused until the occupation of the town. I then obtained permission to leave the department, but General Sherman happened to call on me as I was about starting and urged me so strongly not to think of going, that I concluded to remain.

Halleck was appointed to command of all the Union armies with headquarters in Washington on July 11th. "When General Halleck left to assume the duties of general-in-chief I remained in command of the district of West Tennessee. Practically I became a department commander." So only a month after Sherman had talked him out of leaving the department, Grant had become its commander.

LESSON

The saying, "in time, this too shall pass," holds true even for insufferable bosses. Hang in there. Jumping ship too quickly could cause you to miss a golden opportunity.

71. TEST YOUR ASSUMPTIONS

*I*N JUNE, GRANT HAD TRAVELED WITH HIS STAFF AND A SMALL escort from Corinth to Memphis. A detachment of Confederate cavalry was in the area and could easily have captured Grant. The Confederates were told that Grant and his party had passed the spot where they were standing only three-quarters of an hour earlier.

> *[The Confederate commander] thought it would be useless to pursue with jaded horses a well-mounted party with so much of a start. Had he gone three-quarters of a mile farther he would have found me with my party resting under the shade of trees and without even arms in our hands with which to defend ourselves.*

LESSON

Whenever possible, test your assumptions.

72. USE EVERY POSSIBLE MEANS TO WIN

*W*HILE EN ROUTE TO MEMPHIS, GRANT WAS INVITED TO lunch with a prosperous Southern farmer. The gentleman, who was too old to be in the army himself, pointed with pride to the crops he was raising in support of the rebellion.

I had at the moment an idea that at about the time they were ready to be gathered the "Yankee" troops would be in the neighborhood and harvest them for the benefit of those engaged in the suppression of the rebellion instead of its support.

Grant had been of the opinion that the war could be won with a single decisive military victory, but after the battle of Shiloh, he realized it would take more than success on the battlefield to win the war.

I gave up all idea of saving the Union except by complete conquest. Up to that time it had been the policy of our army, certainly of that portion commanded by me, to protect the property of the citizens whose territory was invaded.... After this, however, I regarded it as humane to both sides to protect the persons of those found at their homes, but to consume everything that could be used to support or supply armies.... Supplies within the reach of Confederate armies I regarded as much contraband as arms or ordnance stores. Their destruction was accomplished without bloodshed and tended to the same result as the destruc-

tion of armies. I continued this policy to the close of the war.... This poli-cy I believe exercised a material influence in hastening the end.

LESSON

Grant believed that it was his duty "to use every means to weaken the enemy, by destroying their means of subsistence, withdrawing their means of cultivating their fields, and in every other way possible." You, too, must use every legal and ethical means at your disposal to insure success.

73. HELP YOUR REPLACEMENT

*W*HEN GENERAL HALLECK WAS TRANSFERRED TO Washington, Grant succeeded him as department head. The day Halleck received his orders, Grant was in Memphis.

He telegraphed me the same day to report at department head-quarters at Corinth. I was not informed by the dispatch that my chief had been ordered to a different field and did not know whether to move my headquarters or not. I telegraphed asking if I was to take my staff with me, and received in reply: "This place will be your headquarters. You can judge for yourself."

Halleck remained at Corinth for a couple of days after Grant's arrival, "but he was very uncommunicative and gave me no information."

LESSON

Even if you can't stand your replacement, you owe it to the organization to help your successor get off to a good start by making the transition as smooth as possible.

74. KNOW HOW TO AGREE TO DISAGREE

*H*ALLECK HAD TREATED GRANT SHABBILY. EVEN SO, WHEN Halleck was ordered to Washington, and before Grant knew that he would be continuing to report to him, he wrote to a friend:

> *He is a man of gigantic intellect and well studied in the profession of arms. He and I have had several little spats but I like and respect him nevertheless.*

LESSON

Good managers know how to disagree without being disagreeable. They can have disagreements and still continue to work well with the people with whom they've disagreed.

75. WHITE ELEPHANTS

*A*FTER TAKING POSSESSION OF CORINTH, GENERAL Halleck had erected fortifications around the town on a massive scale. "They were laid out on a scale that would have required 100,000 men to fully man them.... These fortifications were never used."

After Halleck's departure in July, Grant was free to abandon Halleck's elaborately constructed defense works.

One of the first things I had to do was to construct fortifications at Corinth better suited to the garrison that could be spared to man them. The structures that had been built during the months of May and June were left as monuments to the skill of the engineer, and others were constructed in a few days, plainer in design but suited to the command available to defend them.

LESSON

The first requirement for a physical plant is functionality. Elaborate and costly edifices are nothing more than vainglorious attempts to achieve immortality. Unfortunately, too many organizations that control the design and cost of building and plant construction fail to exercise effective control over systems development. This results in the construction of overly sophisticated systems that are too complicated for end-user production, either because they are too difficult to use or because they break so easily or both.

76. DON'T SCATTER YOUR RESOURCES

*A*FTER THE UNION ARMY OCCUPIED CORINTH, IT WAS Grant's opinion that:

> *[A] force of 80,000 men, besides enough to hold all the territory acquired, could have been set in motion for the accomplishment of any great campaign.... The positive results might have been: a bloodless advance to Atlanta, to Vicksburg, or to any other desired point south of Corinth.*

General Halleck, rather than going on the offensive, chose to disperse his forces, so that when Grant replaced Halleck as the department commander, he discovered that "the magnificent army of 120,000 men which entered Corinth...had now become so scattered that I was put entirely on the defensive in a territory whose population was hostile to the Union."

LESSON

You can't accomplish very much if you scatter your resources and allow yourself to become overextended.

77. TEAR DOWN THE FENCES

*O*PERATING ON THE DEFENSIVE, GRANT SAW AN
opportunity to relieve the pressure on his scattered forces by having the Union troops at Helena, Arkansas carry out a raid on the
Mississippi Central Railroad. But Helena, situated on the
Arkansas bank of the Mississippi River, was not within the bound-
aries of Grant's department, which extended only to the
Mississippi bank of the river.

*Geographical lines between commands during the rebellion were
not always well chosen, or they were too rigidly adhered to.*

During the war, it was not uncommon for some army
department commanders, for reasons that were more often petty
and jealous than high-minded, to refuse to lend support to commanders of other departments.

LESSON

Make it easy for your managers to utilize resources that don't
report to them. Organizations that make it difficult for managers to
use resources not under their direct control are subject to seemingly never-ending turf wars in which both people and projects suffer.

78. DON'T PEE IN YOUR SOUP

*S*HORTLY AFTER BECOMING DEPARTMENT COMMANDER, Grant was informed that the government was going to buy cotton from the Confederacy, and he was to lend assistance to the project. Grant was dumbfounded.

The government wanted to get out all the cotton possible from the South and directed me to give every facility toward that end. Pay in gold was authorized, and stations on the Mississippi River and on the railroad in our possession had to be designated where cotton would be received. This opened to the enemy not only the means of converting cotton into money, which had a value all over the world and which they so much needed, but it afforded them means of obtaining accurate and intelligent information in regard to our position and strength. It was also demoralizing to the troops.

LESSON

Doing business with your competitors is like peeing in your own soup. Unless there truly is no other viable option, you are always better off not to do it. If you must do business with them, their access to your organization must be tightly controlled, while you should seek to learn all you can from the loose-lipped in their organization.

79. ON GIVING SECOND CHANCES

*W*HEN THE FIRING BEGAN AT SHILOH, COLONEL RODNEY Mason had led his regiment off the battlefield. Embarrassed by his performance, he begged Grant to give him another chance.

I felt great sympathy for him and sent him, with his regiment, to garrison Clarksville [Tennessee].... But when he was summoned to surrender by a band of guerillas, his constitutional weakness overcame him. He inquired the number of men the enemy had, and receiving a response indicating a force greater than his own he said if he could be satisfied of that fact he would surrender. Arrangements were made for him to count the guerillas, and [on August 22, 1862]...he surrendered.

Mason also advised his subordinate, who was at Donelson with a smaller force than Mason had at Clarksville, to surrender. But when the guerillas arrived at Donelson, Mason's subordinate "marched out to meet them and drove them away."

LESSON

You always have to put the good of the organization ahead of your personal feelings. Sometimes the initial mistake a person makes is of such a nature, or the potential consequences to the organization from a future screw-up are so grave, that no matter how much you want to, you cannot afford to give that person a second chance.

80. LEARN FROM YOUR MISTAKES

A MONTH AFTER MASON SURRENDERED, COLONEL R. C. Murphy, who had been detailed to guard supplies at Iuka, Mississippi, evacuated the town without resistance upon the approach of Confederate forces. Murphy's commanding officer wanted to courtmartial the Colonel, but Grant overruled him and gave Murphy another chance. Three months later, Grant wished that he hadn't.

General [Earl] Van Dorn appeared [on December 20, 1862] at Holly Springs [Mississippi], my secondary base of supplies, captured the garrison of 1,500 men commanded by Colonel Murphy...and destroyed all our munitions of war, food and forage. The capture was a disgraceful one [since Murphy had surrendered without a fight].

LESSON

In giving Murphy a second chance, Grant repeated the same mistake he had made with Mason. If you don't learn from your mistakes, you'll keep making the same ones again and again.

81. DON'T SQUIRREL AWAY YOUR BEST PEOPLE

*I*N SEPTEMBER, GRANT SENT GENERAL GORDON GRANGER'S division to Louisville, Kentucky to reinforce General Buell. As Granger's division moved out, Grant was disappointed to see that General Philip Sheridan was going with them. Sheridan had been made a brigadier general in July for having routed an enemy force three times the size of his own. Grant was unhappy at the prospect of losing the services of so promising an officer.

I expressed surprise at seeing him and said that I had not expected him to go. He showed decided disappointment at the prospect of being detained. I felt a little nettled at his desire to get away and did not detain him.... His departure was probably fortunate, for he rendered distinguished services in his new field.

LESSON

You can't squirrel away your best people. It's bad for the organization, it's bad for them, and in the long run, it's bad for you.

82. PLAN FOR SUCCESS

*W*HEN THE CONFEDERATES RETREATED FROM THE FIELD AT Shiloh, Grant had failed to pursue them.

I wanted to pursue, but had not the heart to order the men who had fought desperately for two days, lying in the mud and rain whenever not fighting.

The reinforcements that General Buell had brought had arrived after the end of the first day's fighting, and were in better condition to pursue the Confederates. However, Grant had neglected to give Buell orders to do so, and when he and Buell did meet on the battlefield it was already too late in the day "to get troops ready and pursue with effect."

LESSON

You need to plan for success. If you fail to follow up on your successes, your victories will be hollow and impermanent.

83. ON HAVING PLANS AND FAILING TO EXECUTE THEM

*I*N OCTOBER 1862, WHEN CONFEDERATE FORCES UNDER General Van Dorn attempted to capture Corinth, Grant gave instructions before the battle began as to what should be done when it ended.

General Rosecrans, however, failed to follow up the victory, although I had given specific orders in advance of the battle for him to pursue the moment the enemy was repelled.

LESSON

Not having plans to follow up is bad; having plans and failing to execute them is even worse.

84. TIMING IS EVERYTHING

*A*S SOON AS GRANT LEARNED THAT ROSECRANS HAD FAILED to pursue the retreating Confederates, he repeated his order.

> *Rosecrans did not start in pursuit till the morning.... Two or three hours of pursuit on the day of the battle...would have been worth more than any pursuit commenced the next day could have possibly been.*

Grant understood the importance of timing. He had, eight months earlier, attacked Fort Donelson without waiting for reinforcements.

> *I was very impatient to get to Fort Donelson because I knew the importance of the place to the enemy and supposed he would reinforce it rapidly. I felt that 15,000 men on the 8th [of February 1862] would be more effective than 50,000 a month later.*

LESSON

Timing is everything. Late is not always better than never. Getting a late start can turn a promising project into a useless exercise.

85. LEADERS AND FOLLOWERS

*F*OR FAILING TO OBEY HIS ORDERS, GRANT DECIDED TO replace Rosecrans. Before Grant could do so, Rosecrans was appointed to command of a separate department.

I was delighted at the promotion of General Rosecrans to a separate command, because I still believed that when independent of an immediate superior the qualities which I...credited him with possessing, would show themselves. As a subordinate I found that I could not make him do as I wished, and had determined to relieve him from duty.

LESSON

Some people are better leaders than followers.

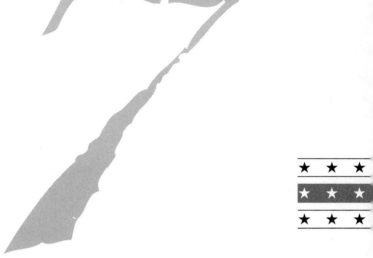

7

SHATTER
PARADIGMS

January ~ October 1863

The Confederate stronghold at Vicksburg holds the key to control of the Mississippi River; its capture would split the Confederacy in two, but there is general agreement that Vicksburg will never fall into Union hands. Grant secures the surrender of the 30,000 men defending Vicksburg by executing a paradigm shift.

86. CREATE ALLIES

*B*EGINNING WITH HIS MOVEMENT AGAINST FORT Donelson, and continuing throughout the war, Grant viewed the Navy as an invaluable resource. He always consulted freely with and listened carefully to his navy counterparts. Grant recalled that Admiral David Porter was the first person with whom he discussed his plans for the final phase of the campaign to capture Vicksburg, Mississippi. "The co-operation of the navy was absolutely essential to the success (even to the contemplation) of such an enterprise. I had no more authority to command Porter than he had to command me." After the surrender of Vicksburg, Grant rode in with the troops, "and went to the river to exchange congratulations with the navy upon our joint victory."

The navy under Porter was all it could be, during the entire campaign. Without its assistance the campaign could not have been successfully made with twice the number of men engaged. It could not have been made at all, in the way it was, with any number of men without such assistance. The most perfect harmony reigned between the two arms of the service. There never was a request made, that I am aware of, either of the flag officer or any of his subordinates, that was not promptly complied with.

LESSON

Treat those who don't report to you as valued allies. Explain the reasons for your requests and solicit their ideas. You not only need to sell them on your plans, you need to give them the opportunity to play a role in their formulation. Above all, if you are unstinting in praising their efforts and assign them a generous share of the credit for your success, you will go a long way toward insuring their future cooperation.

$\mathcal{87.}$ WHEN TO TAKE CHARGE YOURSELF

$\mathcal{O}$RIGINALLY, GENERAL MCCLERNAND WAS TO HAVE LED the expedition to capture the Confederate fortress city of Vicksburg. But Grant "received messages from both Sherman and Admiral Porter, urging me to come and take command in person, and expressing their distrust of McClernand's ability and fitness for so important and intricate an expedition." Grant would have liked to put Sherman in command, but McClernand was the senior major general after Grant, and Sherman was his junior. Grant felt he needed to see for himself what the story was, and so he went to visit McClernand.

It was here made evident to me that both the army and the navy were so distrustful of McClernand's fitness to command that, while they would do all they could to insure success, this distrust was an element of weakness. It would have been criminal to send troops under these circumstances into such danger.... Nothing was left, therefore, but to assume the command myself.

LESSON

Managers who do not enjoy the confidence of their peers or their subordinates cannot be effective. They should not be entrusted with important assignments, even if the only alternative is for you to take charge yourself.

88. WHEN YOU CAN TURN THE OTHER CHEEK AND WHEN YOU CANNOT

*M*cCLERNAND TOOK EXCEPTION TO GRANT'S ASSUMING command.

> *His correspondence with me on the subject was more in the nature of a reprimand than a protest. It was highly insubordinate, but I overlooked it, as I believed, for the good of the service.*

About two weeks before the Confederates in Vicksburg surrendered, both Generals Sherman and McPherson wrote to Grant:

> *...saying that their respective commands had complained to them of a fulsome, congratulatory order [written by McClernand] to the 13th corps, which did great injustice to the other troops engaged in the campaign. This order had been sent North and published, and now papers containing it had reached our camps.... I at once wrote to McClernand, directing him to send me a copy of this order. He did so, and I at once relieved him from the command of the 13th army corps and ordered him back to Springfield, Illinois. The publication of his order in the press was in violation of War Department orders and also of mine.*

LESSON

You can turn the other cheek and overlook personal affronts, but you cannot look the other way when someone is openly and willfully disobedient.

89. MOMMY, DADDY, WHAT ARE YOU DOING? WHY?

*W*HEN GRANT SET OUT TO CAPTURE VICKSBURG, HE TOOK his twelve-year-old son with him.

My son accompanied me throughout the campaign and siege, and caused no anxiety either to me or to his mother, who was at home. He looked out for himself and was in every battle of the campaign. His age, then not quite thirteen, enabled him to take in all he saw, and to retain a recollection of it that would not be possible in more mature years.

LESSON

Not all work environments are appropriate for children, but whenever possible, take your children to work with you. If you can't explain what you're doing and why to their satisfaction, you'll never be able to explain it to anybody else's.

90. DIVERSIONS

*G*RANT'S FORCES NEAR VICKSBURG WERE BOGGED DOWN BY high waters and incessant rains.

There seemed no possibility of a land movement before the end of March or later, and it would not do to lie idle all this time. The effect would be demoralizing to the troops and injurious to their health.... Thence commenced a series of experiments to consume time, and to divert the attention of the enemy, of my troops and of the public generally.

LESSON

Slow periods bring out the worst in some people. Hard workers, when idle, can become malicious gossips, rumor mongers, and malingerers. If you don't want your organization's effectiveness to suffer, you need to keep your staff busy. As an alternative to idleness, have them work on the projects that normally there is never enough time to do. Even if nothing tangible comes from this, the diversion will serve to keep morale high and skills honed.

91. CULTIVATE A THICK SKIN

*D*URING THE WINTER OF 1863, GRANT'S VICKSBURG campaign was at a standstill.

This long, dreary and, for heavy and continuous rains and high water, unprecedented winter was one of great hardship to all engaged about Vicksburg.... Troops could scarcely find dry ground on which to pitch their tents. Malarial fevers broke out among the men. Measles and small pox also attacked them.... Visitors to the camps went home with dismal stories to relate; Northern papers came back to the soldiers with these stories exaggerated.

Grant knew that he could do nothing but watch his men suffer and endure. He also knew that it was a bad idea to prematurely discuss what he intended to do when troop movements could begin again in the spring.

Because I would not divulge my ultimate plans to visitors, they pronounced me idle, incompetent and unfit to command men in an emergency, and clamored for my removal.... I took no steps to answer these complaints, but continued to do my duty, as I understood it, to the best of my ability.

LESSON

You need to cultivate a thick skin to deal with unwarranted criticism. You also need to go about your business without responding to your critics. Trying to explain the reasons for your actions will not satisfy your critics, but it will distract you from your work. Success is the way to silence criticism.

92. CUT THE RED TAPE

*M*ARY LIVERMORE HEADED A DELEGATION FROM THE Sanitary Commission that visited Grant's headquarters in the winter of 1863. She learned of twenty-one sick soldiers who needed to be discharged from the army and sent home; otherwise, they would surely die. The men could not be discharged because their papers had been misplaced, and the army could not grant discharges to men whose papers were not in proper order.

In desperation, Mary Livermore brought the matter directly to Grant. She saw at once that Grant, who was planning the upcoming campaign, was extremely busy. He told her that the matter was one for the chief medical officer. She explained that she had tried that route to no avail. Grant mumbled and sent her away, but not before she had left him the names of the men who were going to die if not discharged. The next day Grant sent her discharge papers for the men.

LESSON

Don't hesitate to cut through the red tape. Sometimes it's the only way to do the right thing quickly.

93. TAP YOUR PEOPLE'S DIVERSE TALENTS

ONE OF THE PROBLEMS GRANT FACED WAS A SHORTAGE of experienced seamen to man his river boats. He called for volunteers from the army.

Captains, pilots, mates, engineers and deck hands enough presented themselves to take five times the number of vessels we were moving....In this instance, as in all others during the war, I found that volunteers could be found...to meet every call for aid.

LESSON

Every organization has many individuals with highly diverse talents. You need to establish mechanisms that make it easy for those talents to come to the fore when a need arises.

LEAD BY EXAMPLE. Second Lieutenants Grant (left) and Alexander Hays in 1845. During the Civil War, Hays could always be found at the head of his brigade. "With him it was 'Come boys,' not 'Go.'"
(Credit: Library of Congress)

SEIZE OPPORTUNITIES. During the battle for Mexico City (September 13, 1847), Grant saw that by mounting a cannon in a church belfry, he could wreak havoc on the Mexicans defending the gate to the city.
Painting by Emanuel Leutze
(Credit: Library of Congress)

WHAT MATTERS IS EFFECTIVENESS, NOT STYLE. General Winfield Scott, known as Old Fuss and Feathers, brilliantly commanded U. S. forces in the Mexican War.
(Credit: U.S. Army Military History Institute)

STUDY YOUR COMPETITION. Grant had known Confederate General Gideon J. Pillow in Mexico, and he used this knowledge to develop his plan to capture Fort Donelson (February 16, 1862). When a Confederate officer told him that Pillow had escaped, Grant said that he needn't have bothered: "If I had captured him, I would have turned him loose. I would rather have him in command of you fellows than a prisoner."
(Credit: Museum of the Confederacy)

TEACH THE MOST IMPORTANT LESSONS FIRST. Union soldiers learn to drill.
(Credit: National Archives)

SEE THE TOTAL PICTURE.
(Credit: Library of Congress)

MAKE ALLIES OF THOSE WHO DON'T REPORT TO YOU.   These Union navy ships played an important part in Grant's victory at Shiloh (April 6-7, 1862).
(Credit: U.S. Army Military History Institute)

AN INSUFFERABLE BOSS.
General Henry W. Halleck, of whom Lincoln's Secretary of the Navy, Gideon Welles, wrote: "Halleck originates nothing; anticipates nothing; takes no responsibility; suggests nothing; is good for nothing."
(Credit: Illinois State Historical Library)

NEW TECHNOLOGY IS NOT A PANACEA. Union soldiers inflate an observation balloon.
(Credit: U.S. Army Military History Institute)

DOING BUSINESS WITH YOUR COMPETITORS IS LIKE PEEING IN YOUR SOUP. During the war, the Union purchased cotton from the Confederacy.

(Credit: Library of Congress)

SEE FOR YOURSELF WHAT'S HAPPENING. Lincoln in the field with General McClellan and his staff.

(Credit: National Archives)

RECOGNIZE WHEN ADDITIONAL RESOURCES WON'T HELP. Confederate General Joseph E. Johnston wisely decided not to attempt to break Grant's siege of Vicksburg.

(Credit: National Archives)

SHATTER PARADIGMS. The Union flag flies over the court house in Vicksburg (July 4, 1863). Grant captured the Confederate fortress city by breaking the paradigm that an army had to operate from a base of supplies.

(Credit: Old Court House Museum, Vicksburg, MS)

THE ONLY COLOR WORTH NOTING IS THE COLOR OF A PERSON'S PERFORMANCE.
Company E, 4th U. S. Colored Infantry.

(Credit: U.S. Army Military History Institute)

POUNCE ON YOUR COMPETITORS' BLUNDERS. Grant smokes a cigar on Lookout Mountain. By taking advantage of his opponent's mistakes, Grant was able to drive the Confederates from their seemingly impregnable positions on the heights above Chattanooga.

(Credit: National Archives)

94. NEVER CAST PLANS IN CONCRETE

GRANT HAD PLANNED TO FIRST COOPERATE WITH GENERAL
Nathaniel Banks in the capture of Port Hudson, Louisiana. Then,
reinforced by Banks' troops, Grant would move against
Vicksburg. But Banks was delayed in moving his forces from the
Red River to Port Hudson.

*The news from Banks forced upon me a different plan of campaign
from the one intended. To wait for his co-operation would have detained
me at least a month.... The enemy would have strengthened his position
and been reinforced by more men than Banks could have brought. I
therefore determined to move independently of Banks.*

LESSON

Never cast your plans in concrete. Leave yourself the flexibility to
improvise your way around unanticipated events.

95. KEEP YOUR EYE ON THE BALL

*O*NCE VICKSBURG AND PORT HUDSON WERE CAPTURED, the Union would control the Mississippi River from its source to its mouth. To Grant, this was the object of the campaign, so when General Banks, who was still on the Red River, wrote to Grant asking for reinforcements, Grant refused to send him any.

I looked upon side movements as long as the enemy held Port Hudson and Vicksburg as a waste of time and material.

LESSON

Avoid chasing after little successes, no matter how appealing or how easily accomplished, that do not aid you in achieving your primary objective. Systems managers frequently fall into the trap of thinking that the implementation of a dozen minor changes more than makes up for their failure to provide the organization with a badly needed, significant new capability. Don't mistake a flurry of quick-fix activity for real progress in systems or in any other part of your organization.

96. EMPIRE BUILDERS

*I*N ADVANCING ON VICKSBURG, GRANT ENCOUNTERED HEAVY resistance outside of Port Gibson, Mississippi (May 1, 1863). During the day's fighting, Grant kept getting messages from General McClernand.

McClernand...sent me frequent requests for reinforcements, although the force with him was not being pressed. I had been upon the ground and knew it did not admit of his engaging all the men he had.

LESSON

Some managers act as if they can never have enough people working for them, irrespective of how many it really takes to do the job. This problem is endemic to some systems managers, who truly seem to believe that all their problems would be solved if only they had more programmers and analysts.

97. OCCASIONALLY GO INTO THE TRENCHES

*A*FTER CAPTURING PORT GIBSON, GRANT'S FORCES needed to rebuild a bridge that the retreating Confederates had burned.

Colonel J. H. Wilson, a member of my staff, planned and superintended the construction of this bridge, going into the water and working as hard as anyone engaged. Officers and men generally joined in this work.

LESSON

It's good for morale if on occasion the manager rolls up his or her sleeves, goes down into the trenches, and does some "real work." Sometimes, it's the only way to get a critically important job done in a hurry. But if "on occasion" becomes a regular occurrence, that's a clear signal the manager is failing.

98. SUCCESSFUL MANAGERS HAVE ENORMOUS STAMINA

*G*RANT REACHED GRAND GULF, MISSISSIPPI ON MAY 3RD. That evening, he went aboard Admiral Porter's flagship.

I had not been with my baggage since the 27th of April and consequently had had no change of underclothing, no meal except such as I could pick up sometimes at other headquarters, and no tent to cover me. The first thing I did was to get a bath, borrow some fresh underclothing from one of the naval officers and get a good meal on the flagship.

After conferring with Admiral Porter, Grant then:

...wrote letters to the general-in-chief informing him of our present position, dispatches to be telegraphed from Cairo [Illinois], orders to General [Jeremiah] Sullivan commanding above Vicksburg, and gave orders to all my corps commanders. About twelve o'clock at night I was through my work and started for Hankinson's ferry, arriving there before daylight.

LESSON

To be a successful manager, you need enormous stamina. You also need to be willing, when necessary, to put forth extraordinary effort and make personal sacrifices.

99. YOU NEEDN'T BE A WORKAHOLIC

*W*HILE GRANT COULD WORK AS LONG AND AS HARD AS anyone else when necessary, he was not a workaholic. When told that Napoleon only required four hours sleep to function effectively, Grant replied:

If the truth were known, I have no doubt it would be found that he made up for his short sleep at night by taking naps during the day.

I am a confirmed believer in the restorative qualities of sleep, and always like to get at least seven hours of it, though I have often been compelled to put up with much less.

LESSON

While extraordinary efforts are occasionally required for extended periods, you don't need to be a workaholic to be successful. Even when you are working under tight time constraints, always try to get a good night's sleep. A fatigued person is both inefficient and error-prone.

100. SHATTER PARADIGMS

*B*EFORE GRANT'S VICKSBURG CAMPAIGN, ALL OF THE armies engaged on both sides of the war had operated "from a base of supplies which they always covered and guarded in all forward movements.... [I] had no idea of the possibility of supplying a moving column in an enemy's country from the country itself."

After the Confederates destroyed his supply base at Holly Springs in December 1862, Grant ordered that all the food and forage within a fifteen-mile radius be collected for the use of his army.

I was amazed at the quantity of supplies the country afforded. It showed that we could have subsisted off the country for two months.... This taught me a lesson which was taken advantage of later in the [Vicksburg] campaign when our army lived twenty days with the issue of only five days' rations by the commissary. Our loss of supplies was great at Holly Springs, but it was more than compensated for by those taken from the country and the lesson taught.

Grant had seen that it might be possible to shatter a cherished paradigm. He would "cut loose from my base [of supplies], destroy the rebel force in rear of Vicksburg and invest or capture the city."

Sherman, who later would cut loose from his bases of supply and march an even larger army through Georgia and the Carolinas, was convinced that Grant's plan would have disastrous consequences. He went to see Grant. "He said it was an axiom of war that when any great body of troops moved against an enemy they should do so from a base of supplies, which they would guard as they would the apple of the eye." Sherman proposed withdrawing to Memphis, establishing a supply depot, and then moving out from there.

To this I replied, the country is already disheartened over the lack of success on the part of our armies...and if we went back so far as Memphis it would discourage the people [even more].... The problem for us was to move forward to a decisive victory, or our cause was lost.

LESSON

When you propose a paradigm shift, even your brightest and most competent subordinates may look aghast. But if breaking the old paradigm allows you to do what up until now was considered impossible, you may by going ahead be able to make all the difference.

101. SUSPEND THE RULES

*G*RANT'S PLANS FOR THE CAPTURE OF VICKSBURG WERE based on his assumption that he could supply the men and animals in his army with food from the country through which they would be moving. However, the army would have to carry its own ammunition.

I directed...that all the vehicles and draft animals, whether horses, mules, or oxen, in the vicinity should be collected and loaded to their capacity with ammunition. Quite a train was collected...and a motley train it was.... The making out of provision returns [receipts for confiscated property] was stopped for the time. No formalities were to retard our progress until a position was secured when time could be spared to observe them.

LESSON

Sometimes you need to suspend the rules. For example, you will rarely have the luxury to fully document new procedures or systems before they're put in place. To insist on doing so would almost certainly delay their implementation. Remember, it is better to have a successful project and tie up the loose ends afterwards, than to deliver a neatly wrapped failure.

102. WHEN THE INFORMATION IS INADEQUATE

*A*T THE BATTLE OF CHAMPION'S HILL, ON MAY 16, 1863, General John Logan's division was in control of a road that Logan and Grant would later discover was the only road over which the Confederate forces could retreat.

Neither Logan nor I knew that we had cut off the retreat of the enemy. Just at this juncture a messenger came from [one of my other division commanders, General Alvin] Hovey, asking for more reinforcements.... I then gave an order to move...[Logan's division] to Hovey.

By moving Logan's division, Grant opened a hole through which the Confederate forces escaped.

LESSON

It's easy to make poor decisions with inadequate information.

103. SEEING MOUNTAINS INSTEAD OF MOLEHILLS

URING THE BATTLE, GENERAL MCCLERNAND, WITH two divisions, was only a few miles from the battlefield. Grant sent McClernand repeated orders to advance and bring his troops into battle.

But he did not come. It is true, in front of McClernand there was a small force of the enemy...obstructing his advance.

LESSON

Managers who treat every minor obstacle as if it were a large mountain to be scaled find it difficult to make progress. Frequently, they have trouble even getting started.

104. WHEN TO DISOBEY ORDERS

*D*URING THE BATTLE AT THE BIG BLACK RIVER BRIDGE ON May 17th, a staff officer arrived with a letter from General Halleck.

It ordered me to return to Grand Gulf and to co-operate from there with [General] Banks against Port Hudson, and then to return with our combined forces to besiege Vicksburg. I told the officer that the order came too late, and that Halleck would not give it now if he knew our position. The bearer of the dispatch insisted that I ought to obey the order, and was giving arguments to support his position when I heard great cheering to the right of our line and, looking in that direction, saw [General Michael] Lawler in his shirt sleeves leading a charge upon the enemy. I immediately mounted my horse and rode in the direction of the charge, and saw no more of the officer who delivered the dispatch; I think not even to this day.

LESSON

There are times when it is appropriate to disobey orders. However, such instances are rare and usually occur only when a manager cannot communicate with his or her boss.

105. THERE ISN'T ONLY ONE RIGHT WAY

*B*EFORE RETREATING INTO THEIR DEFENSES AT VICKSBURG, the Confederates burned the bridge over the Big Black River.

As the bridge was destroyed and the river was high, new bridges had to be built.... Orders were given for the construction of three bridges.... My recollection is that [Lieutenant] Hains built a raft bridge; [General] McPherson a pontoon, using cotton bales in large numbers, for pontoons; and that [General] Ransom felled trees on opposite banks of the river, cutting only on one side of the tree, so that they would fall with their tops interlacing in the river, without the trees being entirely severed from their stumps. A bridge was then made with these trees to support the roadway.

LESSON

There is usually more than one way to get any job done. Managers who always insist that there is only one right way stifle the creative talents of their people.

106. FOOD IS IMPORTANT

$\mathcal{O}$N MAY 19, 1863, GRANT'S FORCES WERE IN POSITION ON the outskirts of Vicksburg.

Most of the army had now been for three weeks with only five days' rations issued by the commissary. They had an abundance of food, however, but began to feel the want of bread.

As Grant was moving through his lines on May 21st, his soldiers let him know they wanted bread in no uncertain terms by shouting "hardtack" at him.

I told the men nearest to me that we had been engaged ever since the arrival of the troops in building a road over which to supply them.... By the night of the 21st all the troops had full rations issued to them. The bread and coffee were highly appreciated.

LESSON

Don't underestimate the importance of your food service or its impact on employee morale.

107. WHEN A QUICK SUCCESS IS UNREALISTIC

*H*AVING FORCED THE CONFEDERATES BACK INTO THEIR defenses at Vicksburg, Grant ordered an assault on the city's fortifications. This attack, which occurred on May 22nd, was a complete failure and resulted in heavy Union losses. Grant knew that the Confederates were in such strong defensive positions that it would probably not be possible to take the city by storm, but he had such good reasons for wanting a quick victory that he decided to attack anyway. He was concerned that a Confederate army might come to the aid of the forces trapped inside Vicksburg. Also, "the immediate capture of Vicksburg would save sending me the reinforcements which were so much wanted elsewhere."

There was no telling how long a regular siege might last.... It was the beginning of the hot season in a Southern climate. There was no telling what the casualties might be among Northern troops working and living in trenches, drinking surface water filtered through rich vegetation, under a tropical sun. If Vicksburg could have been carried in May, it would not only have saved the army the risk it ran of a greater danger than from the bullets of the enemy, but it would have given us a splendid army...to operate elsewhere with.

LESSON

Don't let the allure of a quick success, no matter how desirable, blind you to the realities of the situation. Simply believing you can do the impossible won't make it so, even if you have the best of reasons for wanting to.

108. RECOGNIZE CHANGED CIRCUMSTANCES

*G*RANT WROTE THAT ANOTHER REASON FOR HIS ORDERING the unsuccessful attack was that his troops believed they could take the city by storm.

> *The Army...had won five successive victories...in the three preceding weeks.... [They] had come to believe that they could beat their antagonist under any circumstances.*

But the Union victories had been won against an enemy in the field, not when the Confederates were behind massive fortifications.

LESSON

You need to be able to recognize when circumstances have changed and no longer favor success. Good managers don't send their staff on fools' errands.

109. IN THE AFTERMATH OF A DISASTER

FTER HIS ASSAULT FAILED, GRANT "DETERMINED UPON A regular siege.... As long as we could hold our position the enemy was limited in supplies of food, men and munitions of war to what they had on hand. These could not last."

In this, Grant felt that he did derive one advantage from his failed attempt to storm the city.

The only benefit we gained—and it was a slight one for so great a sacrifice—was that the men worked cheerfully in the trenches after that, being satisfied with digging the enemy out.

LESSON

There is usually some thread of a silver lining to be found in the aftermath of even the worst disasters. Take what solace you can from it, but don't kid yourself into thinking that it justifies the disaster or exculpates you.

110. WHEN TO PUSH SOMEONE AND WHEN NOT TO

*I*N ORDER TO SUCCESSFULLY BESIEGE VICKSBURG, GRANT needed defensive fortifications that would enable his troops to repel attacks by both the Confederates defending the city and those who might try to come to their aid. For the construction of these works, Grant "directed that all officers who had graduated at West Point, where they had necessarily to study military engineering, should in addition to their other duties assist in the work."

Grant's chief commissary was a West Point graduate.

[He] begged off, however, saying that there was nothing in engineering that he was good for unless he would do for a sap roller.... As we would be sure to lose him if he was used as a sap roller, I let him off. The general is a large man; weighs two hundred and twenty pounds, and is not tall.

LESSON

You need to know when to push people into doing jobs they are reluctant to tackle and when not to. But don't ever ask someone to do a job that he or she is physically incapable of doing.

111. WHEN ADDITIONAL RESOURCES WON'T HELP

*G*RANT HAD PREPARED DEFENSIVE FORTIFICATIONS AGAINST the possibility that General Joseph E. Johnston, one of the South's most able commanders, would attempt to come to the rescue of the Confederate forces trapped in the city.

We were strong enough to have taken the offensive against him; but I did not feel disposed to take any risk of losing our hold upon [Vicksburg]...while I would have rejoiced at the opportunity of defending ourselves against an attack by Johnston.

The Confederate defenders at Vicksburg were completely cut off. If Johnston did not come to their aid, they would be forced to surrender. Johnston decided not to attack.

Johnston evidently took in the situation and wisely, I think, abstained from making an assault on us because it would simply have inflicted loss on both sides without accomplishing any result.

LESSON

There is no point in continuing to pour resources into a failed or fatally flawed enterprise. Any hopes of resurrecting it are bound to be forlorn.

112. IF YOU EMPOWER YOUR STAFF

*W*HEN THE SIEGE BEGAN, GRANT'S ARMY HAD ONLY A small number of siege guns and no mortars whatsoever.

Wooden ones were made by taking logs of the toughest wood that could be found, boring them out for six or twelve pound shells and binding them with strong iron bands.... Shells were successfully thrown from them into the trenches of the enemy.

LESSON

Necessity is truly the mother of invention. Your staff will find the way to get the job done if you empower them to do so.

113. CREATIVE EXPLANATIONS

*D*URING THE SIEGE, GRANT FREQUENTLY WROTE TO General Halleck suggesting that General Rosecrans, who was commanding the Union forces in middle and eastern Tennessee, take the offensive against the Confederates under General Braxton Bragg.

General Halleck strongly approved the suggestion and finally wrote me that he had repeatedly ordered Rosecrans to advance, but that the latter had constantly failed to comply with the order, and at last, after having held a council of war, had replied in effect that it was a military maxim "not to fight two decisive battles at the same time".... It would be bad to be defeated in two decisive battles fought the same day, but it would not be bad to win them.

LESSON

Some managers can come up with creative explanations for not carrying out your directions. If the reason smells fishy, don't tolerate it.

114. IT'S NOT A DEMOCRACY

 *G*RANT DIDN'T BELIEVE IN HOLDING "COUNCILS OF WAR."

I believe it is better for a commander charged with the responsibility of all the operations of his army to consult his generals freely but informally, get their views and opinions, and then make up his mind what action to take, and act accordingly.

LESSON

It's critically important to get input from your staff before making a decision, but you abdicate your managerial responsibilities by putting decisions to a vote.

115. THE ONLY COLOR WORTH NOTING

*O*N APRIL 22, 1863, GRANT HAD ISSUED AN ORDER regarding the formation of black regiments.

It is expected that all commanders will especially exert them-selves...not only in organizing colored regiments and rendering them efficient, but also in removing prejudice against them.

Grant's newly recruited black soldiers did not have long to wait before they came under fire.

On the 7th of June [1863] our little force of colored and white troops across the Mississippi, at Miliken's Bend, were attacked by about 3,000.... This was the first important engagement of the war in which colored troops were under fire. These men were very raw, having all been enlisted since the beginning of the siege, but they behaved well.

LESSON

The only color worth noting is the color of a person's performance.

116. READ YOUR COMPETITORS' PUBLICATIONS

*S*TEALING YOUR COMPETITORS' SECRETS IS AN ILLEGAL business practice, but it is a necessity in war, and Grant tried to take full advantage of the information furnished to him by Union spies. He also read the Southern newspapers, since even in wartime most intelligence is gathered through public access channels, although not all of this information is reliable or useful. In his memoirs, Grant recalled reading a humorous passage in the Vicksburg newspaper shortly before the city surrendered on July 4, 1863.

The Vicksburg paper, which we received regularly through the courtesy of the rebel pickets, said prior to the fourth, in speaking of the "Yankee" boast that they would take dinner in Vicksburg that day, that the best recipe for cooking a rabbit was "First ketch your rabbit."... The last [edition of the paper]...was issued on the fourth and announced that we had "caught our rabbit."

If the Vicksburg paper wasn't helpful, speeches made by the Confederate President, Jefferson Davis, in September 1864, after Sherman's army captured Atlanta, were invaluable.

These speeches of Mr. Davis were not long in reaching Sherman. He took advantage of the information they gave, and made all the preparations possible for him to make to meet what now became expected, attempts to break his communications.

LESSON

Not all of the information your competitors publish will be useful to you, but a careful analysis of their quarterly and annual letters and reports to shareholders, filings and reports to regulatory bodies, customer correspondence, advertising, brochures, catalogs, and other marketing material will provide a wealth of valuable information to aid you in assessing their current activities, future plans, and prospects. Conference and technical meeting presentations by competitors and press stories about your competitors also provide grist for your analytical mill.

117. ON REACHING AGREEMENTS

*W*HEN GENERAL JOHN C. PEMBERTON, WHO WAS
commanding the Confederate forces trapped within Vicksburg,
approached Grant about surrendering the city, Grant's initial
response was that "unconditional surrender" were the only terms
that he was willing to offer. On reflection, Grant realized that if
he insisted upon an unconditional surrender, he would have to
transport over thirty thousand prisoners to the East coast at considerable inconvenience to his army (which would have to guard
them for the first part of their journey) and at great expense to
the government. He then made the following proposal to
Pemberton.

*I will march in one division as a guard, and take possession at
eight A.M. tomorrow. As soon as rolls can be made out, and paroles
signed by officers and men, you will be allowed to march out of our lines.*

To Pemberton, surrendering with the "honors of war" was
an important issue. He responded to Grant:

*...in justice both to the honor and spirit of my troops, manifested in
the defense of Vicksburg.... At ten o'clock A.M. tomorrow, I propose
to...surrender by marching out with my colors and arms, stacking them
in front of my present lines. After which you will take possession.*

To this Grant replied:

*If you mean by your proposition for each brigade to march to the
front of the lines now occupied by it, and stack arms at ten o'clock A.M.,*

and then return to the inside and there remain as prisoners until properly paroled, I will make no objection to it.

LESSON

Agreements are reached when each party thinks it has cut the best deal it can. A bargain is when each party thinks it has gotten the better of the other. One of the best ways to insure that the party you are negotiating with thinks it is getting a bargain is to yield on symbolic issues that are important to the other party but have no substantive impact on the results of the negotiation.

118. WHEN NOT TO HOLD A STAFF MEETING

*H*AVING ALREADY MADE UP HIS MIND THAT HE WOULD allow the Confederates to be paroled and not insist upon their unconditional surrender, but before he had communicated this to Pemberton, Grant called a meeting of all his corps and division commanders.

I informed them...that I was ready to hear any suggestion; but would hold the power of deciding entirely in my own hands.

Despite the almost unanimous recommendation of his subordinates that he insist upon the unconditional surrender of Vicksburg, Grant proceeded to propose the more generous terms he had previously decided to offer. By so doing, he sowed seeds of dissatisfaction among his staff and opened himself up to criticism for his actions.

LESSON

There is no purpose in holding a staff meeting to get input on a decision that you've already made. If your mind is already made up and no amount of suasion will change it, then don't carry out a charade. Use the meeting to announce to your staff what you intend to do and to solicit their support.

119. SHAGGY DOG STORIES

*G*RANT KNEW THAT PEMBERTON'S DEMORALIZED TROOPS would desert and go home at the first opportunity. They would never again be an effective fighting force. Pemberton himself wrote to the Confederate President, Jefferson Davis, that he could count on fewer than 2,000 of the over 30,000 who had been paroled. So when a delegation went to Lincoln to demand that Grant be relieved of duty for failing to insist on the unconditional surrender of Pemberton's army, Lincoln told them the story of Sykes dog.

It seems that Mr. Sykes had a large, mean dog that was giving the boys in the neighborhood fits. One day, the boys decided to take care of the dog once and for all. They wrapped a charge of powder in a piece of meat, and when the dog woofed it down, they lit the fuse. Moments later there was a loud explosion. Mr. Sykes came running out of his house to find pieces of his dog falling to the ground. Picking up one of the larger pieces, he said, "Ain't gonna be of much use anymore, not as a dog that is." Lincoln then concluded by telling the delegation that Pemberton's army, like Sykes' dog, wasn't going to be of much use anymore.

Lincoln was an effective storyteller. As he explained:

They say I tell a great many stories. I reckon I do; but I have learned from long experience that plain people, take them as they run,

are more easily influenced through the medium of a broad and humor-
ous illustration than in any other way.

LESSON

Tell stories. A good anecdote, quote, or story can frequently get across the point you are trying to make far more effectively than any other form of explanation. Criticism is easier to swallow when it's dished out in a story, because stories are excellent vehicles for getting your message across without becoming confrontational or personal.

120. SUCCESS IS THE BEST MORALE BOOSTER

*W*HEN THE CONFEDERATES DISPLAYED WHITE FLAGS ON their battlements, the effect was electrifying.

It was a glorious sight to officers and men on the line where these white flags were visible, and the news soon spread to all parts of the command. The troops felt that their long and weary marches, hard fighting, ceaseless watching by night and day, in a hot climate, exposure to all sorts of weather, to diseases and, worst of all, to the gibes of many Northern papers that came to them saying all their suffering was in vain, that Vicksburg would never be taken, were at last at an end.

LESSON

Nothing boosts morale so much as success.

121. KNOW WHEN TO LEAD AND WHEN TO FOLLOW

*D*URING THE CAMPAIGN, GENERAL FRANCIS BLAIR, JR. commanded a division. A former Congressman, Blair would go on to run as the Democratic Party's vice presidential candidate in 1868 against a Republican ticket headed by Grant, and later he would serve in the United States Senate. Blair had been commissioned a major general without having served in a lower grade. When Grant learned that Blair was to be assigned to his command, he dreaded the thought of having to deal with this pure politician turned instant general.

I knew from experience that it was more difficult to command two generals desiring to be leaders than it was to command one army officered intelligently and with subordination. It affords me the greatest pleasure to record now my agreeable disappointment in respect to his character. There was no man...who obeyed all orders of his superior in rank with more unquestioning alacrity. He was one man as a soldier, another as a politician.

LESSON

Many people will rise to the occasion if given the opportunity to do so. Be careful not to prejudge them for past behavior under different circumstances. Your best managers are those who know when to lead and when to follow, and know how to do both well.

122. THE SUPERIOR TEAM PLAYER

*S*HERMAN HAD OPPOSED GRANT'S PLANS FOR THE CAMPAIGN to capture Vicksburg. He had gone to see Grant and had tried to convince him to adopt a different plan. When Grant told Sherman that he would not change his plans, Sherman had written a letter asking Grant to seek the advice of his other key subordinates and laying out Sherman's own proposed plan for the campaign. Grant not only did not heed Sherman's advice, he never even replied to his letter. Sherman's ego had to have been bruised by Grant's behavior. He had been Grant's senior; now his counsel was being ignored and he was being asked to carry out a plan that he believed would fail. Sherman must have felt deeply hurt. But after Vicksburg surrendered, Grant had nothing but praise for Sherman's performance during the campaign.

His untiring energy and great efficiency during the campaign entitle him to a full share of all the credit due for its success. He could not have done more if the plan had been his own.

LESSON

Going along with your boss, after you've let him or her know that you disagree with the decision, is expected. Putting your ego aside and embracing that decision as though it were your own, and then pulling out all the stops to implement it and make it a success, is the hallmark of a truly superior team player.

123. MASTER DETAIL—DON'T DROWN IN IT

*S*HERMAN BELIEVED THAT GRANT DESERVED ALL THE credit for the victory. In his memoirs, Sherman wrote:

The campaign of Vicksburg, in its conception and execution, belonged exclusively to General Grant, not only in the great whole, but in the thousands of its details. I still retain many of his letters and notes, all in his own handwriting, prescribing the routes of march for divisions and detachments, specifying even the amount of food and tools to be carried along.... No commanding general of an army ever gave more of his personal attention to details.

LESSON

Never lose sight of the big picture in the details, but never overlook the details that are critical to the success of your operation. A good manager masters detail without wallowing in it or being overcome by it.

124. PREPARATION FOR PROMOTION

*G*RANT WROTE THAT THE VICKSBURG CAMPAIGN HAD READIED a number of officers for promotion.

Men who thought a company was quite enough for them to command properly at the beginning, would have made good regimental or brigade commanders; most of the brigade commanders were equal to the command of a division, and one...would have been equal to the command of a corps at least.... [Two division commanders] ended the campaign fitted to command independent armies.

LESSON

Nothing prepares a person for promotion so well as working for top-flight individuals on well-managed projects.

125. TO SUCCESSFULLY COMPLETE A LARGE PROJECT

*A*S SOON AS HE LEARNED THAT THE GARRISON AT Vicksburg had surrendered and its 30,000 men were prisoners of war, the Confederate commander at Port Hudson also surrendered. The object of Grant's campaign had been achieved—the Mississippi, from its source to its mouth, was in Union hands. It was an awesome achievement.

The enemy had at Vicksburg, Grand Gulf, Jackson, and on the roads between these places over sixty thousand men. They were in their own country, where no rear guards were necessary. The country is admirable for defense, but difficult for the conduct of an offensive campaign. All their troops had to be met. We were fortunate, to say the least, in meeting...at Port Gibson, seven or eight thousand; at Raymond, five thousand; at Champion's Hill, twenty-five thousand; at the Big Black, four thousand.

Grant defeated an army larger than his own because he took the Confederates on piecemeal.

LESSON

The only way to successfully complete a large project is to first break it into steps; next assign responsibility for achieving the milestones in each step within defined limits of time, cost, and quality; and then take it one step at a time. Many managers allow themselves to be overwhelmed by the seeming enormity of certain tasks; but when those tasks are cut into bite-sized mouthfuls, they are quite doable.

126. IF OFFERED AN ASSIGNMENT YOU DON'T WANT

A FTER VICKSBURG SURRENDERED, SECRETARY OF WAR Stanton suggested that Grant be brought East and given command of the Army of the Potomac. Grant made it clear that this was an assignment he did not want, and that being ordered to command the Army of the Potomac "would cause me more sadness than satisfaction."

> *Here I know the officers and men and what each General is capable of.... There I would have all to learn. Here I know the geography of the country and its resources. There it would be a new study. Besides more or less dissatisfaction would necessarily be produced by importing a General to command an Army already well supplied with those who have grown up, and been promoted, with it.... Whilst I would disobey no order I should beg very hard to be excused before accepting that command.*

LESSON

If you are offered an assignment that you do not wish to accept, don't be afraid to give your reasons for not wanting the job, but don't exaggerate and don't get emotional. Otherwise your words could come back to haunt you if you do end up having to accept the assignment.

127. SAVE YOUR "NO'S"

*I*N EARLY AUGUST 1863, GRANT REQUESTED LEAVE TO VISIT New Orleans. General Halleck initially refused to grant his request.

So far as my experience with General Halleck went it was very much easier for him to refuse a favor than to grant one.

LESSON

Save your "no's" for when you really need them. Don't waste them on insignificant matters, and never use them to remind your staff that you are the boss. The indiscriminate use of "no" is demoralizing.

128. LET THEM WALK IN YOUR SHOES

*I*N EARLY SEPTEMBER, GRANT WAS BADLY INJURED IN A FALL.

When I regained consciousness I found myself in a hotel near by with several doctors attending me.... I lay at the hotel something over a week without being able to turn myself in bed.

While I was absent General Sherman...was glad to render any assistance he could. No orders were issued by my staff, certainly no important orders, except upon consultation with and approval of Sherman.

LESSON

You need to make it clear to your subordinates and everyone else in the organization who will be in charge when you are away or incapacitated, and to the person filling in for you, the degree of freedom that he or she will have in exercising your responsibilities. For your scheduled absences, like vacations, try to rotate the assignment of covering for you among your direct reports. Not only is it wonderful training for them, it gives you the opportunity to see how they handle your job and it avoids the problem of prematurely signaling who your successor is likely to be.

129. BECAUSE WE'VE ALWAYS DONE IT THAT WAY

*G*RANT DID NOT BELIEVE THAT ANY RULES SHOULD BE immutable or any prerogatives irrevocable.

It is preposterous to suppose that the people of one generation can lay down the best and only rules of government for all who are to come after them, and under unforseen contingencies. At the time of the framing of our constitution....the application of steam to propel vessels against both wind and current, and machinery to do all manner of work had not been thought of. The instantaneous transmission of messages around the world by means of electricity would probably...have been attributed to witchcraft.... We could not and ought not to be rigidly bound by the rules laid down under circumstances so different.

LESSON

Organizations that are unable to embrace change are doomed. "Because we've always done it that way" is one of the two most debilitating answers a manager can give in response to a "Why" question from a subordinate. You should immediately remove from management anyone who uses this lazy, non-thinking, stifling phrase.

130. BECAUSE I SAID SO

*G*RANT TRIED NEVER TO ISSUE ORDERS WITHOUT EXPLAINING
the rationale for them. As an example, look at this order he sent
to General McClernand during the Vicksburg campaign:

> *It is evidently the design of the enemy to get north of us.... We
> must not allow them to do this. Turn all your forces...."*

LESSON

Never say, "Because I said so." It is the other of the two most debilitating phrases a manager can use. Explaining the reasons for your
directions serves a twofold purpose: It provides an opportunity for
you and your subordinates to critically reexamine the thought
process that led to your decision, and by so doing, it increases the
probability that your orders will receive your subordinates' wholehearted support.

131. NEGATIVISM

*G*RANT WAS DEEPLY OFFENDED BY THE NORTHERNERS WHO were so highly critical of the war effort that their words both demoralized his men and gave aid and comfort to the enemy.

I always admired the South, as bad as I thought their cause, for the boldness with which they silenced all opposition and all croaking, by press or by individuals, within their control. War at all times...ought to be avoided, if possible with honor. But, once entered into, it is too much for human nature to tolerate an enemy within their ranks.

LESSON

There is a limit to how much dissent an organization can tolerate and still function effectively. Recommendations for change deserve careful consideration no matter who makes them, but there are some in every organization who believe that management always has its head in the sand and can't do anything right. Managers are frequently tolerant of these chronic complainers so long as their work is satisfactory; however, when their bad attitude begins to demoralize others and have an adverse effect upon the organization, then they have to be helped to change their ways or, failing that, to find another job.

POUNCE
ON YOUR COMPETITORS'
BLUNDERS

October 1863 – March 1864

The Union army, defeated at Chickamauga, is trapped in Chattanooga: Its only options appear to be starvation or surrender. Grant assumes command and, by taking advantage of his opponent's blunders, is able to drive the Confederates from their commanding and seemingly impregnable positions on the heights above Chattanooga.

132. PAY ATTENTION TO ALL OF YOUR RESPONSIBILITIES

*I*N OCTOBER 1863, GRANT WAS APPOINTED TO COMMAND OF the newly created Military Division of the Mississippi. His expanded responsibilities now included Chattanooga, where General Rosecrans' army, after its defeat at Chickamauga, was besieged. Grant immediately replaced Rosecrans with General George Thomas.

Grant then sent a telegraph message to Thomas "to hold Chattanooga at all hazards, informing him at the same time that I would be at the front as soon as possible. A prompt reply was received from Thomas, saying, 'We will hold the town till we starve'.... It looked, indeed, as if but two courses were open: one to starve, the other to surrender or be captured."

Grant then

...telegraphed to [General Ambrose] Burnside... that important points in his department ought to be fortified; to Admiral Porter...requesting him to send a gunboat to convoy [supplies for Sherman's army]; and to Thomas, suggesting that large parties should be put to work on the wagon-road then in use back to Bridgeport [Alabama].

LESSON

Even if one of your units is in serious trouble, requiring your immediate and personal attention, you cannot ignore your other responsibilities. If you don't continue to at least give them the attention they minimally require, they'll also turn sour, and you will find yourself having to fight fires on multiple fronts.

133. TEACH PUBLIC RELATIONS

STOPPING BRIEFLY IN NASHVILLE, GRANT MET ANDREW Johnson, who would later succeed Lincoln as President but who was then the Union Governor of Tennessee.

He delivered a speech of welcome.... It was long, and I was in torture while he was delivering it, fearing something would be expected of me in response. I was relieved, however, the people assembled having apparently heard enough. At all events they commenced a general handshaking, which, although trying where there is much of it, was a great relief to me in this emergency.

LESSON

Very few people are natural public speakers. You need to teach effective public relations to your managers before they can be successful at it.

134. DON'T JUST SIT THERE, DO SOMETHING

*O*N HIS WAY TO CHATTANOOGA, GRANT MET BRIEFLY with General Rosecrans, who had been in command there until Grant relieved him.

He described very clearly the situation at Chattanooga, and made some excellent suggestions as to what should be done. My only wonder was that he had not carried them out.

LESSON

There really is no excuse for sitting on your hands, especially when you're up to your ears in a mess of your own making. If you are in charge and have ideas that could help alleviate the situation, act on them. Even if your resources are too limited to drain the swamp, you can at least kill a few of the alligators while waiting for help to arrive.

135. ASK THE RIGHT QUESTIONS

*G*RANT ARRIVED IN CHATTANOOGA ON THE EVENING OF
October 23, 1863. He immediately went to the headquarters of
General George Thomas, who was in command of the Union
forces in the city. "During the evening most of the general officers called in to pay their respects and to talk about the condition
of affairs."

Horace Porter, who would later serve on Grant's staff, was at
Thomas' headquarters that evening. As he recalled:

*General Grant sat for some time as immovable as a rock and as
silent as the sphinx, but listened attentively to all that was said. After a
while he straightened himself up in his chair, his features assumed an
air of animation, and in a tone of voice which manifested a deep interest
in the discussion, he began to fire whole volleys of questions at the officers
present. So intelligent were his inquiries, and so pertinent his suggestions, that he made a profound impression upon every one by the quick-
ness of his perception and the knowledge which he had already acquired
regarding important details of the army's condition.*

LESSON

You won't learn anything while you're doing the talking. If you
wish to learn, you must listen attentively. To learn what you want
to know, you need to ask the right questions; but before you can do
that, you first must do your homework.

136. BUSINESS CORRESPONDENCE

*T*HE FOLLOWING EVENING, GRANT SAT DOWN AND WROTE out orders for the forces under his command. He also informed General Halleck of the moves he was making. These dispatches, like all of Grant's business correspondence, were clear and crisp. Horace Porter described Grant's manner of writing.

He wrote nearly all his documents with his own hand, and seldom dictated to anyone.... His work was performed swiftly and uninterruptedly, but without any marked display of nervous energy....he was never at a loss for an expression, and seldom interlined a word or made a material correction.

In writing his style was vigorous and terse, with little of ornament; its most conspicuous characteristic was perspicuity. General Meade's chief of staff once said: "There is one striking feature about Grant's orders: no matter how hurriedly he may write them...no one ever has the slightest doubt as to their meaning, or ever has to read them over a second time to understand them."

LESSON

Good business correspondence is clear, concise, and to the point.

137. PLANS ALONE ARE NOT ENOUGH

*T*HE SITUATION FOR THE UNION ARMY WAS CRITICAL.

The enemy, with a vastly superior force, was strongly fortified to the east, south, and west, and commanded the river below.... The Union army was short of both [ammunition and medical supplies], not having ammunition enough for a day's fighting.

Braxton Bragg, the Confederate commander, wrote that if the Confederate dispositions were "faithfully sustained, [that would insure] the enemy's speedy evacuation of Chattanooga for want of food and forage.... We held him at our mercy, and his destruction was only a matter of time."

But within a week of Grant's arrival, his troops were receiving full rations, had been resupplied with ammunition, and were being reinforced. Grant attributed this remarkable accomplishment to the failure of the Confederates to faithfully sustain their dispositions.

LESSON

The best-laid plans will come to naught if they are not well executed.

138. DON'T PUT SQUARE PEGS IN ROUND HOLES

*G*ENERAL WILLIAM F. SMITH WAS ACTING AS CHIEF ENGINEER when Grant arrived in Chattanooga.

> *He explained the situation of the two armies and the topography of the country so plainly that I could see it without an inspection. I found that he had established a saw-mill...and completed pontoons and road-way plank for a second bridge, one flying bridge being there already. He was also rapidly getting out the materials...for a third bridge. In addition to this he had far under way a steamer for...whenever we might get possession of the river.*

Before the Civil War, Smith had served as an engineering officer and had been an instructor in engineering at West Point. When Grant was ready to implement the plan to open up a supply line to his besieged troops, he turned to Smith.

> *General W. F. Smith had been so instrumental in preparing for the move which I was now about to make, and so clear in his judgment about the manner of making it, that I deemed it but just to him that he should have command of the troops detailed to execute the design, although he was then acting as a staff officer and was not in command of troops.*

For his contributions to the victory at Chattanooga, Grant had Smith promoted to major general and given command of an army corps. After the battle of Cold Harbor, Smith was ordered to capture Petersburg, Virginia, twenty miles south of Richmond. His failure, on June 15, 1864, to take the virtually defenseless city is generally regarded as a major blunder. Grant was forced to besiege Petersburg, thus killing all hope for a quick end to the war.

LESSON

Just as a super technician is not necessarily a good candidate for supervisor, even the best staff department managers may not be good candidates for general manager jobs. If you are going to move someone from staff to line management, try to do it at an early enough point in his or her career so that the person has adequate opportunities to succeed or fail as a line manager before being placed in a position to take actions that could have calamitous consequences for the organization.

139. SOONER OR LATER EVERYONE GETS SICK

ONE OF THE REASONS GIVEN FOR SMITH'S FAILURE TO capture Petersburg is that he was suffering from a reoccurring bout of malaria, but instead of turning command over to one of his subordinates, he insisted upon taking the field himself, with disastrous consequences.

LESSON

You're not indispensable, so don't act as if you are. Have the good sense to take sick leave if you're ill. Your performance will be below par if you are not physically up to doing the job.

140. SOME PROJECTS NEED TO WAIT

*I*N ADDITION TO BEING WORRIED ABOUT THE FORCES TRAPPED
in Chatanooga, President Lincoln and Secretary of War Edwin
Stanton were very concerned for the safety of General Burnside's
command at Knoxville.

> *Dispatches were constantly coming urging me to do something for*
> *Burnside's relief.... There was no relief possible for him except by [my*
> *first] expelling the enemy from Missionary Ridge and about*
> *Chattanooga.*

LESSON

It's great when you can take on multiple tasks simultaneously, but
there will always be some projects that need to wait until others are
completed. Working on them prematurely only wastes time and
resources.

141. SELF-ASSURED MANAGERS

*G*RANT COULD NOT ATTACK THE CONFEDERATE POSITIONS above Chattanooga until Sherman's troops arrived. On November 13, 1863, the advance guard of Sherman's army reached Bridgeport, Alabama. Sherman went on ahead to Chattanooga, arriving there the evening of the 15th. He immediately went to Grant's headquarters where he was greeted warmly by Grant and several other officers. Grant gave Sherman a cigar and, pointing to a high-backed rocking chair, said:

Take the chair of honor, Sherman.

The chair of honor? Oh no—that belongs to you, General.

Never mind that. I always give precedence to age.

Well, if you put it on that ground I must accept.

Sherman was two years older than Grant.

LESSON

Some managers use the size of their office or where they sit at the conference table as forms of intimidation. Confident, self-assured managers don't worry about where they sit at the table. Because they don't need symbols of power to maintain their authority, they are as likely to visit their subordinates as they are to summon them to their offices.

142. THE NEED FOR URGENCY

*T*HE FOLLOWING DAY GRANT TOOK SHERMAN ON AN inspection tour of the area and explained what was expected of him.

I, as well as the authorities in Washington, was still in a great state of anxiety for Burnside's safety.... Nothing could be done for him, however, until Sherman's troops were up. As soon, therefore, as the inspection was over, Sherman started for Bridgeport to hasten matters, rowing a boat himself.... [He] started back the same evening to hurry up his command, fully appreciating the importance of time.

LESSON

Try to surround yourself with people who understand the need for urgency and act accordingly.

143. HELP IS ON THE WAY

LTHOUGH HE WAS UNABLE TO DO ANYTHING TANGIBLE TO relieve Burnside, Grant sent messages encouraging him to hold on and outlining the plans Grant had developed to come to his assistance. On November 14th, Grant sent Burnside the following telegram:

> *Sherman's advance has reached Bridgeport. His whole force will be ready to move from there by Tuesday at farthest. If you can hold Longstreet in check until he [Sherman] gets up...I will be able to force the enemy back from here and place a force between Longstreet and Bragg that must inevitably make the former take to the mountain-passes.... Sherman would have been here before this but for high water in Elk River driving him some thirty miles up that river to cross.*

LESSON

People can put up with the most intolerable situations—for example, extended systems outages—if they know that help is on the way, the nature of the help they will receive, and when they can expect it. They also need to be given truthful explanations for any delays.

144. WORRYING WON'T HELP

WHILE STILL IN THE PROCESS OF GETTING HIS TROOPS IN position, Grant learned that Burnside's forces had been attacked, and that all communications with Burnside had been cut off.

The President, the Secretary of War, and General Halleck were in an agony of suspense. My suspense was also great, but more endurable, because I was where I could do something to relieve the situation.

LESSON

It's frightening to be in the dark, but biting your nails and pacing the floor won't help. Going about your business and doing your job will.

145. THINGS YOU CAN'T CONTROL

Concerned for Burnside's safety in Knoxville but unable to help him until the Confederates had been driven from their positions above Chattanooga, Grant was nonetheless forced by bad weather to delay his assault. As Grant succinctly put it, "The elements were against us."

[The] rains [were] falling so heavily as to delay the passage of troops over the river at Brown's Ferry and threatening the entire breaking of the bridge.

LESSON

You can't control some things, like the weather, but you can minimize their disruptive effects by keeping them in mind when you make your plans.

146. SHARED PURPOSE

ROOPS FROM THREE SEPARATE UNION ARMIES PARTICIPATED in the battle of Chattanooga. Because of the heavy rains and the rising waters of the Tennessee River, units from one army found themselves temporarily attached to a different army.

There was no jealousy—hardly rivalry. Indeed, I doubt whether officers or men took any note at the time of the fact of this intermingling of commands. All saw a defiant foe surrounding them, and took it for granted that every move was intended to dislodge him, and it made no difference where the troops came from so that end was accomplished.

LESSON

Once imbued with a sense of shared purpose, your managers and their people will happily overlook any necessary departures from organizational norms and will unite to get the job done.

147. IF CHANGING DIRECTION

IN ORDER TO BRING HIS TROOPS INTO POSITION FOR THE
attack on Missionary Ridge, Grant gave orders for General
Joseph Hooker's corps to cross the north face of Lookout
Mountain. Upon reconsidering, Grant changed his mind and
instead ordered Hooker to have his troops cross the Tennessee
River at Brown's Ferry. Grant then changed the orders back to
what they had been originally.

*The original order had to be reverted to, because of a flood in the
river rendering the bridge at Brown's Ferry unsafe for the passage of
troops at the exact juncture when it was wanted to bring all the troops
together against Missionary Ridge.*

LESSON

Your people will think you haven't a clue if you appear to them to
be constantly changing direction, unless you take the time and
make the effort to explain your reasons for each change.

148. ASK FOR EXTRAORDINARY EFFORT

HERIDAN'S DIVISION HAD CHARGED UP MISSIONARY RIDGE (November 25, 1863) in the face of a murderous rain of cannon and musket balls, and had driven the Confederates from their positions. Pushing forward late in the day, Sheridan's exhausted troops encountered a Confederate rear guard occupying a second hill behind Missionary Ridge. After such a hard day's work, Sheridan would not have been criticized for stopping for the night.

It was now getting dark, but Sheridan without halting on that account pushed his men forward up this second hill.... [The enemy] beat a hasty retreat, leaving artillery, wagon trains, and many prisoners in our hands.

LESSON

A good manager knows when to ask his or her people for that last extraordinary effort that makes all the difference.

149. GIVE THE JOB TO SOMEONE ELSE

FTER THE BATTLE, GRANT GAVE ORDERS FOR GENERAL Gordon Granger's corps to march to Knoxville to assist Burnside. After pursuing the retreating Confederates to Ringgold, Georgia, Grant returned to Chattanooga to discover that Granger had not yet left for Knoxville.

Finding that Granger had not only not started but was very reluctant to go, he having decided for himself that it was a very bad move to make, I sent word to General Sherman...and directed him to march to the relief of Knoxville.... I was very loath to send Sherman, because his men needed rest.... But I had become satisfied that Burnside would not be rescued if his relief depended upon General Granger's movements.

LESSON

If one of your subordinates is so opposed to what you have instructed that he or she cannot give the project the wholehearted support it deserves, you will be much better off to give the assignment to someone else.

156. CONGRATULATIONS

*W*ITH THE VICTORY AT CHATTANOOGA AND SHERMAN'S linking up with Burnside at Knoxville, east Tennessee was now securely in Union hands. Lincoln sent Grant a thank-you note.

I wish to tender you, and all under your command, my more than thanks, my profoundest gratitude for the skill, courage, and perseverance with which you and they, over so great difficulties, have effected that important object. God bless you all.

LESSON

A good manager never forgets to give subordinates a pat on the back for a job well done.

151. POUNCE ON YOUR COMPETITORS' BLUNDERS

A MONTH AFTER HIS ARRIVAL IN CHATTANOOGA, GRANT'S troops had driven the Confederate forces from their commanding positions on Missionary Ridge and Lookout Mountain, and won a major victory.

The victory at Chattanooga was won against great odds, considering the advantage the enemy had of position, and was accomplished more easily than was expected by reason of [Confederate General Braxton] Bragg's making several grave mistakes: first, in sending away his ablest corps commander [General James Longstreet] with over twenty thousand troops; second, in sending away a division of troops on the eve of battle; third, in placing so much of a force on the plain in front of his impregnable position.

LESSON

Your competitors' blunders can lead to your greatest successes, if you take advantage of them.

152. GET ALONG WITH YOUR PEOPLE

*G*RANT THOUGHT THAT BRAXTON BRAGG "WAS A REMARKABLY intelligent and well informed man…. But he was possessed of an irascible temper, and was naturally disputatious." Grant tells an anecdote he heard about Bragg to illustrate his point. It seems that as a young officer, Bragg was serving both as post quartermaster and as the commander of a company. As company commander he filled out a requisition for the quartermaster, and as quartermaster he declined to fill his own requisition. As company commander he insisted that the quartermaster fill his requisition, and as quartermaster he continued to refuse to do so. Finally, Bragg referred the matter to the post commander, who, "when he saw the nature of the matter referred, exclaimed: 'My God, Mr. Bragg, you have quarrelled with every officer in the army, and now you are quarrelling with yourself!'"

According to Grant, one possible reason for the absence of General Longstreet at the battle of Chattanooga is that he and his superior, General Bragg, were quarreling, and Jefferson Davis, seeing that he could not resolve the differences between them, had given orders for Longstreet's corps to attack the Union forces at Knoxville.

LESSON

It's not enough to be able to get along with your boss and your peers. You also need to be able to get along with the people who work for you. Otherwise, you won't be able to retain them.

153. MICRODIRECTION FROM THE TOP

*T*HERE IS ANOTHER POSSIBLE EXPLANATION FOR THE DECISION to send Longstreet's corps to Knoxville. Jefferson Davis believed that the Confederates could win simultaneous victories at Chattanooga and Knoxville.

It may be that Longstreet was...sent to Knoxville...because Mr. Davis had an exalted opinion of his own military genius, and thought he saw a chance of "killing two birds with one stone." On several occasions during the war he came to the relief of the Union army by means of his superior military genius.

Grant knew it made no sense whatsoever to send Longstreet away from Chattanooga, because if the Confederates had captured Chattanooga, "Knoxville...would have fallen...without a struggle."

LESSON

Microdirection from the top, by those who are above the highest knowledgeable level, is bad for any organization.

154. TREACHEROUS BEHAVIOR

ONE OF GRANT'S SUBORDINATES AT CHATTANOOGA WAS General Joseph Hooker. Grant felt that Hooker had performed brilliantly, but Grant distrusted Hooker.

I nevertheless regarded him as a dangerous man. He was not subordinate to his superiors. He was ambitious to the extent of caring nothing for the rights of others. His disposition was...to exercise a separate command, gathering to his standard all he could of his juniors.

LESSON

If you have to watch your back because of a subordinate, get rid of him or her. You can't do your job if you're standing with your back to a wall. Even the most brilliant performance doesn't justify treacherous behavior.

155. SUCCESS LEADS TO SUCCESS

*G*RANT BELIEVED THAT EACH VICTORY HIS TROOPS GAINED made it that much easier for them to win the next time.

The fact is troops who have fought a few battles and won, and followed up on their victories, improve upon what they were before to an extent that can hardly be counted by percentage.

LESSON

Success leads to success. Of course, the same is true of failure. Both can be infectious.

156. DON'T PROCRASTINATE

FTER HIS VICTORY AT CHATTANOOGA, GRANT MADE HIS headquarters in Nashville. While there he approved a report recommending some rather costly expenditures. When asked by the officer who presented him with the report if he was certain he was making the right decision, Grant replied:

No, I am not, but...anything is better than indecision. We must decide. If I am wrong we shall soon find it out and can do the other thing. But not to decide wastes both time and money and may ruin everything.

LESSON

It is true that you won't trip or stumble while you're standing still, but you won't make any progress either. Procrastination never solves anything.

157. TAKE RESPONSIBILITY FOR YOUR ACTIONS

*I*N LATE DECEMBER, GRANT TRAVELED TO CHATTANOOGA and Knoxville, returning to Nashville in mid-January 1864. Before leaving on this trip, so as to be able to continue to send encrypted messages to his commanders and to the War Department, Grant ordered the cipher operator at his headquarters in Nashville to turn over the key for encoding and decoding messages to a member of his staff who would be accompanying him on his trip.

The operator refused point blank to turn over the key...stating that his orders from the War Department were not to give it to anybody— the commanding general or anyone else.... He said that if he did he would be punished. I told him if he did not he would most certainly be punished. Finally...he yielded. When I returned from Knoxville I found quite a commotion. The operator had been reprimanded very severely and ordered to be relieved. I informed the Secretary of War [Edwin P. Stanton]...that the man could not be relieved, for he had only obeyed my orders....that they would have to punish me if they punished anybody.

LESSON

Never let someone else take the heat for following your directions.

158. STAND UP FOR YOUR RIGHTS

*L*ATER, AFTER HE HAD BEEN APPOINTED COMMANDING general of all the Union armies, Grant would have another run-in with Secretary of War Stanton.

> *Owing to his natural disposition to assume all power and control in all matters that he had anything whatever to do with, he...prohibited any order from me going out of the adjutant-general's office until he had approved it.... I remonstrated against this in writing, and the Secretary apologetically restored me to my rightful position of General-in-Chief of the Army.*

LESSON

The worst mistake you can make when dealing with a bully, even if the bully is your boss, is to roll over and allow yourself to be pushed around. Don't be afraid or hesitant to stand up for your rights.

159. POWER GRASPERS

GRANT FELT THAT STANTON WAS THE KIND OF MANAGER who was always trying to exceed his authority.

Mr. Stanton never questioned his own authority to command.... He cared nothing for the feelings of others. In fact it seemed to be pleasanter to him to disappoint than to gratify. He felt no hesitation in assuming the functions of the executive [the President], or in acting without advising him.

LESSON

If you have someone working for you who has caught the power-grasping bug, squash it quickly if you can, or dump him or her if you can't. Otherwise, you'll have dissension among your managers.

160. SUCCESSFUL MANAGERS ARE FORCE MULTIPLIERS

*I*N EARLY FEBRUARY, GENERAL WILLIAM SOOY SMITH WITH A force of 7,000 cavalry was ordered to move against Confederate General Nathan Bedford Forrest.

Forrest had about 4,000 cavalry with him, composed of thoroughly well disciplined men, who under so able a leader were very effective. Smith's command was nearly double that of Forrest, but not equal, man to man.... [This] is often due to the way troops are officered, and for the particular kind of warfare which Forrest had carried on neither army could present a more effective officer than he was.

In the series of engagements that followed, Forrest handily defeated Smith.

LESSON

The successful manager gets superior performance from ordinary people.

161. STAY ON THEIR CASE

*W*HEN GRANT LEARNED THAT THE CONFEDERATES WERE planning to send reinforcements to their troops in east Tennessee, he ordered General Thomas to take the important road junction town of Dalton, Georgia, twenty-five miles southeast of Chattanooga.

> *On the 12th of February [1864] I ordered Thomas to take Dalton and...I directed him to move without delay. Finding that he had not moved, on the 17th I urged him again to start, telling him how important it was.... Then again on the 21st, he not yet having started, I asked him if he could not start the next day. He finally got off on the 22d or 23d. The enemy fell back from his front without a battle.*

In December 1864, Grant found himself once again urging Thomas to take the offensive, this time against Confederate General John Bell Hood's army, which was in the vicinity of Nashville.

> *General Thomas' movements being always so deliberate... I consequently urged Thomas in frequent dispatches...to make the attack at once.... It was all without avail further than to elicit dispatches from Thomas saying that he was getting ready to move as soon as he could, that he was making preparations, etc.*

Thomas finally did attack, "and was successful from the start."

LESSON

Conditions are rarely perfect for the initiation of any project. If you have subordinates who have a tendency to delay taking action until they have all their ducks perfectly lined up in a row, you'll need to stay on their case, and in spite of that, you need to anticipate that they will take longer getting off the mark than you would have liked.

162. PLAY TO THEIR STRENGTHS

*G*ENERAL THOMAS HAD BECOME A NATIONAL HERO WHEN HE covered the retreat of the Union troops fleeing from the battle-field at Chickamauga. The sobriquet he earned that day, "the rock of Chickamauga," tells us much about his character. In spite of the difficulties Grant had with Thomas when he was urging him to take the offensive, Grant recognized Thomas' qualities. He knew that for certain tasks, Thomas was the best man for the job.

He possessed valuable soldierly qualities in an eminent degree. He gained the confidence of all who served under him, and almost their love. This implies a very valuable quality. It is a quality which calls out the most efficient services of the troops serving under the commander possessing it.

Thomas's dispositions were deliberately made, and always good. He could not be driven from a point he was given to hold. He was not as good, however, in pursuit as he was in action. I do not believe that he could ever have conducted Sherman's army from Chattanooga to Atlanta against the defenses and the commander guarding that line in 1864. On the other hand, if it had been given him to hold the line which [Confederate General Joseph] Johnston tried to hold, neither that general nor Sherman, nor any other officer could have done it better.

LESSON

A good manager knows the strengths and weaknesses of his or her people and, to the extent possible, gives them assignments that play to their strengths.

FOCUS ON WHAT
YOU COULD BE DOING

March – Mid-June, 1864

Appointed lieutenant general and given command of all the Union armies, Grant develops and implements his strategic plan for ending the war. Sherman will march on Atlanta; Grant will go after Robert E. Lee. When a Union general expresses concern about Lee's intentions, Grant tells him to stop worrying about what Lee might do and instead focus on what he could be doing to Lee.

163. YOU NEED GOOD PEOPLE

On March 3, 1864, Ulysses S. Grant was ordered to report to Washington, D.C. He had been promoted to lieutenant general and given command of all the Union armies. While en route, Grant wrote to Sherman.

While I have been eminently successful in this war...no one feels more than I how much of this success is due to the energy, skill, and the harmonious putting forth of that energy and skill, of those whom it has been my good fortune to have occupying subordinate positions under me.

LESSON

The superior manager knows that the key to success is his or her ability to attract and retain good people and get them to work well together as a team.

164. THE EXECUTIVE SUITE

*I*N HIS LETTER TO SHERMAN, GRANT MADE ONE OTHER POINT.

I shall say very distinctly upon my arrival there that I accept no appointment which will require me to make that city [Washington, D.C.] my headquarters.

LESSON

Too many managers can't wait until they get an office in the executive suite. That may be fine if you're the chairman of the board or the president, but everyone else should be located in a work area. The best way to know what's really happening and insure that the work will be done right is to be where the work is done.

165. ON BECOMING FAMOUS

GRANT AND HIS SON FRED ARRIVED IN WASHINGTON AND went to the Willard Hotel. The desk clerk had seen his share of Union major generals, and the unprepossessing officer in his rumpled, travel-worn uniform, with boy in tow, didn't impress him one whit. The clerk said that he could let Grant have a small room on the top floor. Grant said that would be fine and signed the register. When the clerk turned the register around to write the room number, he saw "U.S. Grant and son, Galena, Ill." The clerk was beside himself. He was looking at the man who had just been made general-in-chief. A small room on the top floor would never do for Lieutenant General Grant. He would get the finest suite, the one that President Lincoln had stayed in prior to his inauguration. With no more emotion than he had shown accepting a small room, Grant said that would be fine and followed the clerk, who insisted on personally carrying Grant's bag, to his suite.

LESSON

With success come the perquisites. Don't let them go to your head. The real measure of your value is the contribution you make. The flatterers who suddenly want to fawn over you because of your new status or prestige should be avoided like the plague.

166. KNOWING WHAT TO DO IS NOT ENOUGH

*I*N TAKING COMMAND OF THE UNION ARMIES, GRANT replaced General Halleck, who became Chief of Staff of the army. Of Halleck, Sherman wrote:

> *I had in him the most unbounded confidence in 1862. He was the best informed scholar of the military art in America.... But war is a terrible test. Halleck did not stand the test; whereas Grant did. Halleck was a theoretical soldier; Grant was a practical soldier.*

LESSON

It's not enough to know what to do; you also need the ability and the will to do it. Even the most brilliant students of management will be failures as managers if they lack the skill to apply what they have learned.

167. YOU CAN'T SUCCEED IF THEY DON'T

AT THEIR FIRST MEETING, PRESIDENT LINCOLN, THE nation's chief executive officer, gave Lieutenant General Grant, the newly appointed chief operating officer for the prosecution of the war, his marching orders. As Grant recalled:

All he wanted...was someone who would take responsibility and act, and call on him for all the assistance needed, pledging himself to use all the power of the government in rendering such assistance.

LESSON

Good managers realize that they cannot succeed if the people working for them are not successful. Therefore, they empower their people and then do everything they can to help insure their success.

168. LOBBYING FOR PROMOTION

*G*RANT HAD NO USE FOR THOSE WHO LOBBIED FOR POSITIONS
of power.

*Every one has his superstitions. One of mine is that in positions of
great responsibility everyone should do his duty to the best of his ability
where assigned by competent authority, without application or use of
influence to change his position.... I having been selected, my responsibility ended with my doing the best I knew how. If I had sought the place
or obtained it through personal or political influence, my belief is that I
would have feared to undertake any plan of my own conception, and
would probably have awaited direct orders from my distant superiors.
Persons obtaining important commands by application or political influence are apt to keep a written record of complaints and predictions of
defeat, which are shown in case of disaster. Somebody must be responsible
for their failures.*

After Grant arrived in Washington, he visited the headquarters of the Army of the Potomac and met with its commander,
General George Meade.

*[Meade] said to me that I might want an officer who had served
with me in the West...to take his place. If so, he begged me not to hesitate about making the change. He urged that the work before us was of
such vast importance to the whole nation that the feeling or wishes of no
one person should stand in the way of selecting the right men for all
positions. For himself, he would serve to the best of his ability wherever
placed.*

*This incident gave me even a more favorable opinion of Meade
than did his great victory at Gettysburg the July before. It is men who*

wait to be selected, and not those who seek, from whom we may always expect the most efficient service.

LESSON

Be wary of those who either directly or through their friends lobby for promotion. People who gain promotion through politics continue to play that game and are always more worried about covering their behinds than getting the job done. Promote only those who are worthy to take on increased responsibilities. Focus solely on each candidate's past performance and what that tells you about his or her prospects for future accomplishments.

169. IF YOU DO THEIR JOBS, YOU WON'T HAVE TIME FOR YOURS

*W*HEN IT WAS SUGGESTED TO GRANT THAT HE SHOULD replace General Meade and take command of the Army of the Potomac himself, Grant replied:

I am commanding all the armies, and I cannot neglect others by giving my time exclusively to the Army of the Potomac, which would involve performing all the detailed duties of an army commander, directing its administration, enforcing discipline, reviewing its court-martial proceedings, etc. I have Burnside's, Butler's and Sigel's armies to look after in Virginia, to say nothing of our western armies.... General Meade...by attending to the details he relieves me of much unnecessary work, and gives me more time to think and to mature my general plans.

As Horace Porter recalled:

[Grant] studiously avoided performing any duty which some one else could do as well or better than he.... He was one of the few men holding high position who did not waste valuable hours by giving his personal attention to petty details.... He held subordinates to a strict accountability in the performance of such duties, and kept his own time for thought.

LESSON

Senior managers need to delegate so that they'll have time to think. Grant believed they should be "possessed of sufficient breadth of view and administrative ability to confine their attention to perfecting their organizations, and giving a general supervision to their commands, instead of wasting their time upon [petty] details."

170. SHUFFLE THE DECK

ONE OF GRANT'S FIRST MOVES WAS TO PLACE SHERIDAN in command of the cavalry corps with the Army of the Potomac. He made the change because of his "dissatisfaction with the little that had been accomplished by the cavalry so far in the war, and the belief that it was capable of accomplishing much more than it had done."

This relieved General Alfred Pleasonton. It was not a reflection on that officer, however, for I did not know but that he had been as efficient as any other cavalry commander.

LESSON

Sometimes you need to bring in new management with a fresh perspective, not because the existing managers have done a bad job, but because they have been at it for so long and are so set in their ways that they no longer see opportunities to take their people's performance to the next level.

171. CARBON COPIES ARE ALWAYS PALE. BE ORIGINAL.

*G*RANT BELIEVED THAT ONE OF THE PROBLEMS THE UNION
had in the early stages of the war was that its generals were trying
to fight the Civil War using the strategy and tactics of the
Napoleonic era.

*They were always thinking about what Napoleon would do.
Unfortunately for their plans, the rebels would be thinking about something else.... Even Napoleon showed that; for my impression is that his
first success came because he made war in his own way, and not in imitation of others.*

LESSON

You will never be successful by trying to slavishly imitate the practices of others. Take what you can of value, meld it with your own
thinking, and apply it to your unique circumstances.

172. THE PLANNING PROCESS

*G*RANT'S FIRST TASK AS GENERAL-IN-CHIEF WAS TO DEVELOP a coherent plan of action. The Union forces were under the direction of "seventeen distinct commanders. Before this time these various armies had acted separately and independently of each other.... I determined to stop this."

Grant's mission was clear—crush the rebellion. To accomplish this, he developed a strategic design that called for a coordinated movement of the Union armies with the primary objective being the destruction of Robert E. Lee's Army of Northern Virginia. To General Meade, commanding the Army of the Potomac, he wrote:

So far as practicable all the armies are to move together, and towards one common centre.... Lee's army will be your objective point. Wherever Lee goes, there you will go also. The only point upon which I am now in doubt is, whether it will be better to cross the Rapidan [River] above or below him. Each plan presents great advantages over the other with corresponding objections.... These advantages and objections I will talk over with you more fully than I can write them.

LESSON

Planning begins by developing the strategic objectives that must be met for the organization to fulfill its mission. Interim goals and the time frames allowed for accomplishing them are then established, and the specific actions that must be taken to achieve each goal are detailed. The planning process, done well, requires considerable effort at all levels of the organization, and is time-consuming. Each proposed objective, goal, and action plan should be critically questioned and alternative courses of action should be carefully reviewed. The planning process is the crucible in which the organization's future is formed. While many of the specific plans an organization develops will need to be modified due to changed circumstances, a well-constructed strategic planning framework will keep the organization properly focused. In a sense, the plans themselves are less important than either the planning process through which they are developed or the invaluable management training that process provides. Of course, the planning process itself needs to be carefully managed; otherwise planning will become an end unto itself.

173. DETAILED PLANNING, I

*T*O GENERAL SHERMAN, GRANT ASSIGNED THE SECONDARY but almost equally important task of destroying General Joseph Johnston's army and capturing the important railroad center of Atlanta. To Sherman, Grant wrote:

> *You I propose to move against Johnston's army, to break it up and to get into the interior of the enemy's country as far as you can, inflicting all the damage you can against their war resources. I do not propose to lay down for you a plan of campaign, but simply lay down the work it is desirable to have done and leave you free to execute it in your own way. Submit to me, however, as early as you can, your plan of operations.*

LESSON

Detailed plans are best developed by the managers who are responsible for carrying them out.

174. DETAILED PLANNING, II

*G*RANT'S LETTER TO SHERMAN DID MORE THAN SPELL OUT Sherman's objective in the upcoming campaign. It detailed the movements to be made by the other Union commanders as well.

For your information I now write you my program, as at present determined upon. I have sent orders to Banks...he is to commence operations against Mobile as soon as he can. Gilmore joins Butler...and the two operate against Richmond from the south side of the James River.... I will stay with the Army of the Potomac, increased by Burnside's corps...and operate directly against Lee's army, wherever it may be found. Sigel collects all his available force...to move against the Virginia and Tennessee Railroad.

LESSON

Detailed plans are best developed in the context of an overall general plan, the major elements of which are known to all the managers involved.

175. EVERYONE NEEDS TO BE INVOLVED

*G*RANT AND MEADE WOULD GO AFTER LEE; SHERMAN WAS to go after Johnston; and as Grant explained to Lincoln, the movements planned for the other Union armies were designed to prevent Lee and Johnston from receiving reinforcements and supplies.

He had of course become acquainted with the fact that a general movement had been ordered all along the line... I explained to him that it was necessary to have a great number of troops to guard and hold the territory we had captured, and to prevent incursions into the Northern States. These troops could perform this service just as well by advancing as by standing still; and by advancing they would compel the enemy to keep detachments to hold them back, or else lay his own territory open to invasion. His [Lincoln's] answer was: "Oh, yes! I see that. As we say out West, if a man can't skin he must hold a leg while somebody else does."

LESSON

You can't afford to have anyone sitting on the sidelines. Everyone in the organization needs to be involved in carrying out your major objectives, and they need to understand the important role they are playing in doing so.

176. EVERYONE IS MORTAL

*I*N DECIDING TO GO AFTER LEE, GRANT KNEW THAT HE would be taking on the most admired commander of the Civil War. General Robert E. Lee's praises were not only sung by the Southern press but by many Northern newspapers. Some Union officers were so afraid of him that in spite of Grant's successes in the West, it was not uncommon for officers in the Army of the Potomac to remind Grant's staff that Grant had yet to meet Bobby Lee.

The natural disposition of most people is to clothe a commander of a large army whom they do not know, with almost superhuman abilities. A large part of the National [Union] army...and most of the press of the country, clothed General Lee with just such qualities, but I had known him personally, and knew that he was mortal; and it was just as well that I felt this.

LESSON

Cultivate a healthy respect for your competitors, but bear in mind that they too put their pants on one leg at a time. Try not to overestimate or underestimate them, and never forget that no matter how highly one or more of them may be regarded, if you make the mistake of holding them in awe, you will lack the will to beat them.

177. UNREALISTIC EXPECTATIONS

*B*EFORE SETTING OUT WITH THE ARMY OF THE POTOMAC to fight Lee's Army of Northern Virginia, Grant let Lincoln know not to expect any quick or easy victories.

Where two such armies meet on common ground, about equal in numbers, and equally well handled, I do not know why any better results should be expected from one than the other.... While I hope and expect to defeat them, I do not know why this war should not end, as wars generally do, by the exhaustion of the strength and resources of the weaker party.

When a reporter asked Grant how long it would take him to get to Richmond, he replied:

I will agree to be there in about four days. That is, if General Lee becomes a party to the agreement. But if he objects, the trip will undoubtedly be prolonged.

LESSON

Guard against unrealistic expectations by your superiors, yourself, and your subordinates. Also, never make predictions to the press.

178. DON'T PREPARE AN ALIBI

*B*EFORE THE START OF GRANT'S VIRGINIA CAMPAIGN, Lincoln said of him:

He doesn't ask me to do impossibilities for him, and he's the first general I've had that didn't. You see, when any of the rest set out on a campaign they'd look over matters and pick out some one thing they were short of and that they knew I couldn't hope to give them and then tell me they couldn't win unless they had it.

Before leaving on the campaign, Grant wrote to Lincoln:

Should my success be less than I desire and expect, the least I can say is, the fault is not with you.

LESSON

Good managers realize that they alone are ultimately responsible for the success or failure of their efforts. They do not establish alibis or look to lay blame on others.

179. YOU CAN'T SHOOT THE LIARS

*D*URING THE INITIAL PHASES OF THE CAMPAIGN, WILLIAM Swinton accompanied Grant's headquarters. Grant was given assurances that Swinton was a historian, but Grant soon discovered that Swinton was a newspaper reporter. He had lied about being a historian, had published confidential information, and had attempted to eavesdrop on private conversations.

General Meade came to my headquarters saying that General Burnside had arrested Swinton...and had ordered him to be shot that afternoon. I promptly ordered the prisoner to be released, but that he must be expelled from the lines of the army not to return again.

LESSON

You can't shoot the liars, snoops, and gossips, but you can get the liars out of your organization. Showing any tolerance for lying sends the worst possible signal to your staff. Also, you must be careful not to share confidences with people who are unable or unwilling to keep them, and you can't afford to be lazy with confidential documents—when not being used, they must be kept under lock and key. You, yourself, of course, must never use lies or half-truths as management tools.

180. COME, NOT GO

URING THE FIGHTING IN THE WILDERNESS, ONE OF Grant's West Point classmates, Alexander Hays, was killed (May 5, 1864) while leading his brigade in battle.

He was a most gallant officer, ready to lead his command wherever ordered. With him it was "Come boys," not "Go."

LESSON

The best first-line supervisors are leaders who practice management by example.

181. SIFT OUT THE TRUTH

*L*ATE IN THE AFTERNOON OF MAY 6TH, CONFEDERATE General Jubal Early successfully attacked troops under the command of General John Sedgwick, capturing several hundred prisoners including two generals.

Many officers, who had not been attacked by Early, continued coming to my headquarters even after Sedgwick had rectified his lines a little farther to the rear, with news of the disaster, fully impressed with the idea that the enemy was pushing on and would soon be upon me.

Horace Porter vividly remembered that night:

Darkness had set in, but the firing still continued. Aides came galloping in.... Some declared that a large force had broken and scattered Sedgwick's entire corps. Others insisted that the enemy had turned our right completely and captured the wagon-train. It was asserted at one time that both Sedgwick and [General Horatio] Wright had been captured.... Without the change of a muscle of his face, or the slightest alteration in the tones of his voice, he [Grant] quietly interrogated the officers who brought the reports; then, sifting out the truth...he gave directions for relieving the situation.

LESSON

You not only need to know which questions to ask, you also need to be able to tell which answers to believe. Some people have a tendency, which can be exacerbated by stress, to exaggerate. Always confirm the accuracy of their comments before taking any action.

182. FOCUS ON WHAT YOU COULD BE DOING

URING THE NIGHT THAT GRANT WAS RECEIVING REPORTS about the "disaster" that had befallen Sedgwick, one of the Union generals expressed grave concerns that Lee would follow up on the Confederate success and move to cut off the Union army. Grant's response was:

> *Some of you always seem to think he [Lee] is suddenly going to turn a double somersault, and land in our rear and on both of our flanks at the same time. Go...and try to think what we are going to do ourselves, instead of what Lee is going to do.*

LESSON

It is important to think about what your competitors may be planning and the impact that could have upon you, but it is even more important to be thinking about what you could be doing yourself.

183. WHEN THE GOING GETS TOUGH

HE UNION AND CONFEDERATE ARMIES HAD GRAPPLED IN the Wilderness. Union losses were as heavy as they had been at the battle of Chancellorsville, fought on nearly the same ground only a year before. Then, the Union troops had been withdrawn back across the Rapidan.

On the evening of May 7th, Grant ordered a night march south to Spotsylvania Court House. As he moved through his lines that night, it became apparent to the troops that instead of retreating they were continuing to advance. Horace Porter remembered that night as one of the most memorable of the war, for as Grant passed by, the men began to cheer.

Wild cheers echoed through the forest.... Men swung their hats, tossed up their arms, and pressed forward to within touch of their chief, clapping their hands and speaking to him with the familiarity of comrades. Pine-knots and leaves were set on fire.... The night march had become a triumphal procession.

LESSON

You will win the affection and respect of your people once they see that you don't quit just because the going gets tough.

184. BE AN EARLY BIRD

*T*HAT SAME EVENING (MAY 7TH), GENERAL LEE ORDERED General Richard Anderson to march his corps to Spotsylvania Court House early on the morning of the 8th, but Anderson, instead of waiting until morning, moved immediately and was able to take possession of Spotsylvania and entrench himself before a significant number of Union troops arrived.

It is impossible to say now what would have been the result if Lee's orders had been obeyed as given; but it is certain that we would have been in Spotsylvania, and between him and his capital. My belief is that there would have been a race between the two armies to see which could reach Richmond first, and the Army of the Potomac would have had the shorter line. Thus...we came near closing the campaign.

LESSON

You won't go wrong by carrying out your instructions promptly, and rarely will you get in trouble for starting a project early, only for completing it late.

185. INSTANT RECOGNITION

ON MAY 10TH, COLONEL EMORY UPTON LED AN ASSAULT that nearly succeeded in overrunning the Confederate defenses in the "bloody angle" at Spotsylvania. Grant acted immediately.

I had been authorized to promote officers on the field for special acts of gallantry. By this authority I conferred the rank of brigadier-general upon Upton on the spot.

LESSON

Those who have made a contribution that goes above and beyond the norm deserve instant recognition and reward, including promotion when appropriate.

186. STAY THE COURSE

ROM THE FIGHTING IN THE WILDERNESS AND AT Spotsylvania Court House, Grant concluded that his hopes for a decisive battle and a quick end to the war were unrealistic. Lee was engaged in a defensive war. He would not risk losing all in a single battle. The campaign was going to be a costly and protracted one. On May 11th, Grant wrote to Halleck:

> *We have now ended the 6th day of very hard fighting...our losses have been heavy as well as those of the enemy.... I am now sending back...all my wagons for a fresh supply of provisions and ammunition, and propose to fight it out on this line if it takes all summer.*

Lincoln told one of his secretaries:

> *How near we have been to this thing before and failed. I believe if any other general had been at the head of that army, it would have [retreated and by] now been [back] on this side of the Rapidan. It is the dogged pertinacity of Grant that wins.*

LESSON

You can't let the setbacks that you encounter deter you from accomplishing your mission. The road to success is rarely smooth going; it takes persistence and tenacity to get there.

187. TOO MUCH OF A GOOD THING

*A*FTER THE BATTLE OF SPOTSYLVANIA, GRANT SENT BACK to Washington over one hundred of his artillery pieces.

The Wilderness and Spotsylvania battles convinced me that we had more artillery than could ever be brought into action at any one time. It occupied much of the road in marching, and taxed the [supply] trains in bringing up forage. Artillery is very useful when it can be brought into action, but it is a very burdensome luxury where it cannot be used.

LESSON

Having too much of a good thing is costly, and it can be harmful if it limits your flexibility or slows your response to changes in your business.

188. NEVER PLAGIARIZE

*G*RANT HAD SENT HIS CHIEF ENGINEER, GENERAL JOHN Barnard, to inspect the positions held by General Benjamin Butler's troops at Bermuda Hundred, Virginia. Barnard reported that while Butler was safe against an attack, he could not move offensively because the Confederates had him bottled up. "As Barnard expressed it, the enemy had corked the bottle and with a small force could hold the cork in place."

This struck me as being very expressive of his position...and in making my subsequent report I used that expression without adding quotation marks, never thinking that anything had been said that would attract attention—as this did, very much to the annoyance, no doubt, of General Butler and, I know, very much to my own.

By failing to use quotation marks, Grant had given much more weight to the issue of Butler's being bottled up than would have been the case had he noted that he was quoting General Barnard.

LESSON

Be careful to give the source of any references you make, not only to give proper credit, but also to avoid adding the weight of your position to someone else's work.

189. PROMOTIONS TO SENIOR MANAGEMENT

*I*N MAY 1864, GRANT WROTE TO SECRETARY OF WAR STANTON recommending a number of promotions, including those of Meade and Sherman. At the time of Grant's recommendation, Sherman, Grant's most trusted general, was leading an independent campaign to capture Atlanta, while Meade was operating as Grant's second in command in Virginia. Sherman had been with Grant at Shiloh, Vicksburg, and Chattanooga. Meade and Grant had only worked together for two months.

He [Meade] and Sherman are the fittest officers for large commands I have come in contact with. If their services can be rewarded by promotion to the rank of Major-Generals in the regular army the honor would be worthily bestowed, and I would feel personally gratified. I would not like to see one of these promotions at this time without seeing both.

LESSON

Promotions to senior management positions must be made in light of the total contribution that each individual candidate has made and can be expected to continue to make. If you are going to be making two promotions, by doing them simultaneously, you avoid speculation about which of the two has the edge over the other.

190. IF YOU SHOOT THE MESSENGERS

*W*HILE GRANT THOUGHT SO HIGHLY OF GENERAL MEADE that he recommended his promotion at the same time he recommended Sherman's, Grant was well aware of Meade's shortcomings.

He was unfortunately of a temper that would get beyond his control, at times, and make him speak to officers of high rank in the most offensive manner. No one saw this fault more plainly than he himself, and no one regretted it more. This made it unpleasant at times, even in battle, for those around him to approach him even with information.

LESSON

If you keep shooting the messengers, they will stop coming.

191. WE ALL MAKE MISTAKES

*O*N JUNE 3, 1864, GRANT ORDERED AN ASSAULT UPON THE entrenched Confederate forces at Cold Harbor. It was his worst mistake of the war.

> *I have always regretted that the last assault at Cold Harbor was ever made.... At Cold Harbor no advantage whatever was gained to compensate for the heavy loss we sustained.*

LESSON

Good managers recognize when they've made a mistake, and they aren't hesitant to admit it and take full responsibility for their actions.

DEVELOP
AN ALTERNATE PLAN

Mid-June 1864 – February 1865

Lee's defensive tactics convince Grant that following his original plan will result in unacceptably high casualties, so Grant develops and implements an alternate plan. Outflanking Lee, he besieges Petersburg, twenty miles south of Richmond. By keeping Lee from sending reinforcements to other quarters, Grant insures Sherman's success at Atlanta and Sheridan's in the Shenandoah Valley.

192. DEVELOP AN ALTERNATE PLAN

*L*EE'S DEFENSIVE TACTICS LED GRANT TO REALIZE THAT continued direct assaults upon the Confederate entrenchments "would cause a slaughter of our men that even success would not justify." He concluded that he would have to modify his plans. As he explained to Halleck:

> *I now find, after over thirty days of trial, the enemy deems it of the first importance to run no risks with the armies they now have. They act purely on the defensive behind breastworks.... Without a greater sacrifice of human life than I am willing to make all cannot be accomplished that I had designed.... I have therefore resolved upon the following plan....*

LESSON

When you realize that the path you're on won't lead to success, or it will but at too great a cost, don't abandon your goal. Instead, develop an alternative approach to get you there.

193. CORRECT PRIOR INJUSTICES

*O*N THE NIGHT OF JUNE 12TH, GRANT BEGAN TO implement his alternate plan. He broke contact with Lee's army, moved his forces to the south bank of the James River and attacked Petersburg. In one of the initial assaults (June 18, 1864) Colonel Joshua Lawrence Chamberlain was severely wounded. Chamberlain, a hero of the battle of Gettysburg, for which he was later awarded a Medal of Honor, "had several times been recommended for a brigadier-generalcy for gallant and meritorious conduct."

On this occasion, however, I promoted him on the spot, and forwarded a copy of my order to the War Department, asking that my act might be confirmed...without any delay. This was done, and at last a gallant and meritorious officer received partial justice at the hands of his government, which he had served so faithfully and so well.

LESSON

Take advantage of every opportunity to correct prior injustices by recognizing and rewarding deserving individuals who have previously been passed over for promotion.

194. DON'T MAKE EXCEPTIONS FOR YOURSELF

After making several unsuccessful attempts to capture Petersburg by storm, Grant laid siege to the city. He established his headquarters at City Point. As Horace Porter recalled, "ample wharves, storehouses, and hospitals were rapidly constructed, and a commodious base of supplies was established in the vicinity."

The day the wharf was completed and planked over the general [Grant] took a stroll along it....and had not gone far when a sentinel called out: "It's against orders to come on the wharf with a lighted cigar." The general at once took his Havana out of his mouth and threw it into the river, saying: "I don't like to lose my smoke, but the sentinel's right. He evidently isn't going to let me disobey my own orders."

Today, Washington, D.C. tour guides tell the story that during Grant's presidency a carriage he was driving was stopped for speeding. When the police officer saw that the driver was the President, he wanted to forget the whole incident, but Grant would not let him. Saying that no one should be above the law, Grant insisted upon being given a ticket, for which he paid the fine.

LESSON

The fewer the rules the better, but the rules should apply equally to everyone. Don't make exceptions for yourself. It's demotivating to your people if you hold them to rules that do not apply to you.

195. BIG FAILURES—LITTLE FAILURES

*G*ENERAL JUBAL EARLY, FINDING HIMSELF TEMPORARILY unopposed in the Shenandoah Valley, moved quickly to attack Washington, which was lightly defended. General Lew Wallace, who had little hope of success given the forces under his command, met Early at the Monocacy River (Maryland) on July 9, 1864.

They met the enemy and, as might have been expected, were defeated; but they succeeded in stopping him for the day on which the battle took place.

Early resumed his march the next day and reached the outskirts of the Capital on the 11th, the same day that reinforcements arrived, forcing Early to retreat.

General Wallace contributed on this occasion, by the defeat of the troops under him a greater benefit to the cause than often falls to the lot of a commander...to render by means of a victory.

LESSON

Not all failures are equally bad, especially little failures that keep you from big ones later.

196. BE CAREFUL WHEN THINKING OUT LOUD

*W*ITH JUBAL EARLY'S FORCES THREATENING WASHINGTON, Grant came under pressure to release his hold on Lee's army at Petersburg and come north to defend the capital. President Lincoln made the following suggestion to Grant:

Now what I think is that you should...retain your hold where you are certainly, and bring the rest with you personally and make a vigorous effort to destroy the enemy's force in [the vicinity of Washington].... This is what I think, upon your suggestion, and it is not an order.

Later that summer, Lincoln read a dispatch that Grant had sent to General Halleck in response to Halleck's concern that the need for troops elsewhere would require Grant to lift the siege of Petersburg. Lincoln sent Grant the following message:

I have seen your dispatch expressing your unwillingness to break your hold where you are. Neither am I willing. Hold on with a bulldog grip, and chew and choke as much as possible.

LESSON

In too many organizations, even the most casual comments of senior managers are treated as gospel. Make sure your subordinates can tell the difference between when you are making a suggestion and when you are giving direction.

197. SHARP-TONGUED MANAGERS

$\mathcal{G}$ENERAL WILLIAM F. SMITH'S IMMEDIATE SUPERIOR WAS General Benjamin Butler. Smith was openly critical of Butler, Meade, and others. Regarding Butler, Smith asked Grant in a letter:

How can you place a man in command of two army corps who is as helpless as a child on the field of battle and as visionary as an opium eater in council.

Shortly after receiving this letter, Grant relieved Smith of his command.

LESSON

Sharp-tongued managers who cannot or will not learn to button their lips in public are usually more trouble than they are worth. There is no place for sarcasm in business correspondence, and nasty comments are nonproductive. Never say something about someone that you wouldn't say to his or her face.

198. WHEN SOMEONE HAS TO GO

*A*FTER GRANT RELIEVED HIM, GENERAL SMITH LOBBIED for another command. Grant would not allow him to have one. As Adam Badeau, one of Grant's aides, said of Grant:

> *He bore with a man whose characteristics would have been intolerable with some superiors, and put up with even ill success or insubordination, sometimes too long; but if once he determined to free himself from an incompetent, or inefficient, or unmanageable lieutenant, he never relented, nor was willing to be embarrassed by the same cause again.*

LESSON

When you finally reach the conclusion that the time has come to let someone go, stick with it.

199. DON'T PUSH YOUR FAVORITES

*W*ITH THE DEATH OF GENERAL JAMES MCPHERSON IN A
battle on the outskirts of Atlanta (July 22, 1864), the command of
McPherson's army fell to General John Logan who performed
well during the remainder of that engagement. Grant had
watched Logan progress from a colonel to a major general and
felt strongly "that he had proved himself equal to all the...posi-
tions which he had occupied." Grant, therefore, was disappointed
when Sherman selected a different general to succeed
McPherson.

*I have no doubt, whatever, that he [Sherman] did this for what he
considered would be to the good of the service...though I doubt whether
he had an officer with him who could have filled the place as Logan
would have done. Differences of opinion must exist between the best of
friends as to policies in war, and of judgment as to men's fitness. The
officer who has command, however, should be allowed to judge of the fitness of the officers under him, unless he is very manifestly wrong.*

LESSON

You can't second-guess your managers' selections for promotion.
You do have an obligation to assure yourself that the performance
of the candidates selected merited promotion, but you can't push
your favorites (no matter how deserving) down your managers'
throats without damaging your organization.

200. EMPOWERING INSTRUCTIONS

*G*RANT REALIZED THAT SINCE HE COULD NOT BE IN MORE than one place at any time, there was a limit to how detailed his orders could be. In December 1862, in ordering Sherman to lead an expedition (which failed) to capture Vicksburg, Grant wrote: "...proceed to the reduction of that place in such manner as circumstances, and your own judgment, may dictate." When Burnside's position in Knoxville was threatened, Grant provided general guidance, but as to the specifics, he wrote: "Being there, you can tell better how to resist Longstreet's attack than I can direct."

In preparing for an assault on Petersburg, Grant recalled that he "gave Meade minute orders on...how I wanted the assault conducted." But because some of Meade's corps commanders had the tendency to react to Confederate actions rather than to seek out ways to take the initiative, even Grant's detailed instructions contained these empowering sentences:

One thing, however, should be impressed on corps commanders. If they see the enemy giving way on their front or moving from it...they should take advantage of such knowledge and act promptly without waiting for orders.

LESSON

With some people, you need only give general direction. With others you must be specific in your empowering instructions.

201. PICKING THE RIGHT PERSON FOR THE JOB

*O*N JULY 30, 1864, IN ONE OF THE MOST REPORTED events during the siege of Petersburg, a large mine was exploded under the Confederate fortifications. The explosion was a complete success and created a huge crater, but the Union assault that followed was a colossal failure. The fault lay with the corps commander, General Burnside, who failed to follow Grant's instructions regarding preparations for the assault; and even more so with the division commander chosen to lead the assault, General James H. Ledlie, a craven coward who hid in the rear while his leaderless troops were slaughtered when they became trapped in the crater created by the explosion. Grant had given Meade detailed instructions for the assault; Meade had expanded on these in the directions he gave to his subordinates.

Meade's instructions...were all that I can see now was necessary. The only further precaution which he could have taken...would have been to have different men to execute them.

L E S S O N

There is no more important task for a manager than the selection and assignment of managers.

202. MAKE SURE THE WORK IS DONE PROPERLY

*A*BOUT THE FAILURE OF THE ASSAULT THAT FOLLOWED THE explosion of the mine, Grant said:

> *I think if I had been a corps commander...I would have been down there and would have seen that it was done right; or, if I had been the commander of the division that had to take the lead, I think I would have gone in with my division.... I think the cause of the disaster was simply leaving the passage of orders from one to another down to an inefficient man. I blame his seniors also for not seeing that he did his duty, all the way up to myself.*

LESSON

The first thing a manager learns is that it's his or her responsibility to see that the work is done properly by others.

203. FOLLOW-UP

ON AUGUST 1ST, GRANT WROTE TO HALLECK TELLING him to put Sheridan in command of the Union troops in the Shenandoah Valley. Sheridan's instructions were to get south of the Confederate forces and give them no respite. The Shenandoah Valley, the last great storehouse available to the Confederates for feeding Lee's army, was to be laid waste. But Grant's instructions were counter to Secretary of War Stanton's desire to keep the Union forces in the Valley north of the Confederates, so as to always have troops between the enemy and Washington. Lincoln, on seeing Grant's instructions to Halleck, sent the following message to Grant:

I have seen your dispatch in which you say, "I want Sheridan put in command of all the troops in the field, with instructions to put himself south of the enemy, and follow him to the death. Wherever the enemy goes, let our troops go also." This, I think, is exactly right.... But please look over the dispatches you may have received from here, even since you made that order, and discover, if you can, that there is any idea in the head of anyone here, of "putting our army south of the enemy," or of "following him to the death," in any direction. I repeat to you it will neither be done nor attempted unless you watch it every day, and hour, and force it.

LESSON

Good managers know how much follow-up is required to insure that their instructions are carried out to their liking.

204. WHEN TO LOOK FOR ANOTHER JOB

*G*IVING SHERIDAN COMMAND OF ALL THE TROOPS IN THE
Shenandoah Valley was a slap in the face to General David
Hunter, whose department included the Valley. Grant informed
Hunter that he should "establish the headquarters of the depart-
ment at any point that would suit him best, Cumberland,
Baltimore, or elsewhere, and give Sheridan command of the
troops in the field."

*The general replied to this, that he thought he had better be
relieved entirely. He said that...[his superiors] seemed so much to distrust
his fitness for the position he was in that he thought somebody else ought
to be there.... There were not many major-generals who would volun-
tarily have asked to have the command of a department taken from
them on the supposition that for some particular reason, or for any reason, the service would be better performed.*

LESSON

If you've lost the confidence of your superiors and can't regain it,
it's time to find another job.

205. AN OVERDEVELOPED SENSE OF CAUTION

*I*N MID-AUGUST 1864, GRANT HAD LEE'S ARMY TIED DOWN defending Petersburg and Richmond, Sheridan had been given command of the troops in the Shenandoah, and Sherman was on the outskirts of Atlanta. General Halleck, with his characteristic display of caution, wrote to Grant.

He...advised taking in sail, and not going too fast.

Within a month of receiving Halleck's advice, Atlanta had been occupied by Sherman's army, and Sheridan was winning victories in the Shenandoah.

LESSON

An overdeveloped sense of caution can cost you opportunities for success. If you focus only on the obstacles, you will lose sight of the goal.

ASK FOR EXTRAORDINARY EFFORT. Confederate cannon captured by the Union soldiers who charged up Missionary Ridge (November 25, 1863).
(Credit: Library of Congress)

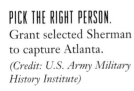**PICK THE RIGHT PERSON.**
Grant selected Sherman
to capture Atlanta.
*(Credit: U.S. Army Military
History Institute)*

RESPECT YOUR COMPETITORS BUT DO NOT FEAR THEM. The last time Robert E. Lee wore his Confederate uniform was to pose for this picture, requested by Queen Victoria.

(Credit: National Archives)

FOCUS ON WHAT YOU COULD BE DOING. Grant concentrates on writing an order while Confederate artillery shells burst overhead.

Drawing by Benjamin West Clinedinst, in *Century Magazine*, April 1897

(Credit: Library of Congress)

SELF ASSURED MANAGERS DON'T NEED TO SIT AT THE HEAD OF THE TABLE. Grant and his officers at Massaponax, Virginia (May 21, 1864).

(Credit: U.S. Army Military History Institute)

DON'T SEND YOUR STAFF ON FOOLS' ERRANDS.

(Credit: Library of Congress)

ADMIT YOUR MISTAKES.
Grant after the costly
and futile assault at Cold
Harbor (June 3, 1864).

*(Credit: U.S. Army Military
History Institute)*

WHERE YOU STAND AFFECTS WHAT YOU SEE. Grant watches the Union army cross the James River (June 1864).

Drawing by Benjamin West Clinedinst, in *Century Magazine*, April 1897
(Credit: Library of Congress)

DEVELOP AN ALTERNATE PLAN. Unable to win a decisive victory over Lee, Grant altered his plan and attacked Petersburg (June 15, 1864). A Union artillery battery shells the city.

(Credit: Library of Congress)

MAKE SURE THE WORK IS DONE PROPERLY. Grant wrote that the failure of the assault through this crater, created by the explosion of a mine under the Confederate fortifications at Petersburg (July 30, 1864), was "the saddest affair I have ever witnessed in the war."

(Credit: U.S. Army Military History Institute)

YOU NEED GOOD PEOPLE TO SUCCEED. Lincoln holds a staff meeting with Sherman (left), Grant and Admiral David D. Porter (March 27-28, 1865).
Painting by George Peter Alexander Healy
(Credit: White House Collection)

TREAT EVERYONE WITH DIGNITY AND RESPECT. Grant proposed generous terms for the surrender of Lee's army at Appomattox (April 9, 1865).
Lithograph by Major & Knapp, 1867
(Credit: Library of Congress)

YOU CAN'T STOP THE CLOCK. The last photograph of Grant, taken four days before his death on July 23, 1885.

(Credit: Library of Congress)

MERGER, NOT CONQUEST. The Blue and the Gray at the 50th anniversary of the battle of Gettysburg (1913).

(Credit: Library of Congress)

206. KEEP YOUR SUBORDINATES CURRENT

*A*S THE GENERAL COMMANDING ALL OF THE UNION armies, Grant was in regular communication with army commanders in other parts of the country. He did not limit his communications only to their activities, but always made a point of trying to keep them informed about what was happening in all the active theaters of operation. For example, on September 12th, Grant sent the following letter to Sherman:

> *I send Lieutenant-Colonel Porter, of my staff, with this. Colonel Porter will explain to you the exact condition of affairs here better than I can do in the limits of a letter. Although I feel myself strong enough for offensive operations, I am holding on quietly to get advantage of recruits and convalescents, who are coming forward very rapidly.... I propose, when I do move, to extend my left.... At the same time this move is made, I want to send a force...against Wilmington [North Carolina]. The way I propose to do this is to....*

LESSON

It's not sufficient to involve your subordinates in planning. The total picture keeps changing as significant plans and events unfold. You need to make sure your subordinates are kept abreast of current developments, including those in areas for which they have no direct responsibility. By doing so, you will enhance their sense of belonging to a team. By keeping them current, you also give them the opportunity to modify their plans in light of changed overall circumstances.

207. PRIDE OF AUTHORSHIP

*G*RANT MET WITH SHERIDAN ON SEPTEMBER 16TH. HE wanted Sheridan to attack the Confederate forces and drive them out of the Shenandoah Valley. Sheridan was to leave such a trail of devastation that the Valley would no longer be able to serve as a source for the resupply of Lee's army.

I asked him [Sheridan] if he had a map showing the positions of his army and that of the enemy. He at once drew one out of his side pocket.... He said that if he had permission he would move so and so (pointing out how) against the Confederates, and that he could "whip them." Before starting [out to meet Sheridan] I had drawn up a plan of campaign for Sheridan, which I had brought with me; but, seeing that he was so clear and so positive in his views and so confident of success, I said nothing about this and did not take it out of my pocket.

LESSON

Don't allow yourself to be hung up over pride of authorship. It doesn't matter whose plan you use, so long as the plan selected leads to success. Whenever possible let your managers work the plans that they have developed. They will have greater confidence in and make a greater commitment to achieving the success of their own plans than someone else's.

208. UNPLEASANT JOBS

*G*RANT'S PLAN FOR THE SHENANDOAH VALLEY WAS GRIM. The Union troops were to "eat out Virginia clear and clean as far as they go, so that crows flying over it for the balance of the season will have to carry their provender with them." After he gained possession of the Valley, Sheridan carried out his assignment to reduce it to "a barren waste."

Sheridan went to work...gathering in the crops, cattle, and everything...required by our troops; and especially taking what might be of use to the enemy. What he could not take away he destroyed.

LESSON

Not all jobs are equally pleasant, but if it's your job to do, then do it completely and do it well.

209. THINK LEAN

*S*HERIDAN'S CAMPAIGN IN THE SHENANDOAH VALLEY WAS enormously successful.

> *Sheridan having driven the enemy out of the valley, and taken the productions of the valley so that instead of going there for supplies the enemy would have to bring his provisions with him if he again entered it, recommended a reduction of his own force, the surplus to be sent where it could be of more use.*

LESSON

Superior managers take every opportunity to reduce the size of their staff to no more than the minimum number of people required to do the job well. They do not build empires or use head count as a status symbol.

210. WHEN TO GO SLOWLY

GENERAL JOSEPH JOHNSTON HAD FOUGHT A BRILLIANT defensive campaign against Sherman's superior forces. "He husbanded his men and saved as much of his territory as he could, without fighting decisive battles in which all might be lost." Desiring a decisive victory, Jefferson Davis replaced Johnston with General John Bell Hood, an action that pleased Grant and Sherman no end. Hood's "policy was to fight the enemy wherever he saw him, without thinking much of the consequences of defeat." As a result, Atlanta fell to Sherman much more quickly and easily than would have been the case had Johnston been left in command.

For my own part, I think that Johnston's tactics were right. Anything that could have prolonged the war a year beyond the time that it did finally close, would probably have exhausted the North to such an extent that they might then have abandoned the contest and agreed to a separation.

LESSON

When the odds do not favor a quick success, it is foolish to try to achieve one. Sometimes the best path to follow is a slow, unglamorous one.

211. A SOLID STRING OF SUCCESSES

HERMAN'S FORCES OCCUPIED ATLANTA ON SEPTEMBER 2, 1864, thereby assuring Lincoln's reelection. Grant was elated. From his perspective, the campaign to capture Atlanta "was one of the most memorable in history. There was but little if anything in the whole campaign...to criticize at all, and nothing to criticize severely. It was creditable to the general who commanded and the army which had executed it."

The news of Sherman's success reached the North instantaneously and set the country aglow.... It was followed later by Sheridan's campaign in the Shenandoah Valley; and these two campaigns probably had more effect in settling the election...than all the speeches, all the bonfires, and all the parading.

LESSON

While a solid string of successes is no guarantee of protection against the vagaries of organizational politics, it is the best remedy available to ward off their evils.

212. DON'T BE JEALOUS

*W*HEN SHERMAN CAPTURED ATLANTA, GRANT WROTE TO him:

I feel that you have accomplished the most gigantic undertaking given to any general in this war with a skill and ability which will be acknowledged in history as unsurpassed, if not unequalled. It gives me as much pleasure to record this in your favor as it would in favor of any living man, myself included.

After Sherman's army had marched across Georgia and captured Savannah, there was talk in Congress of promoting Sherman to lieutenant general and having him replace Grant, who was still bogged down outside of Petersburg, as commander of all the Union forces. Sherman wrote to his brother, Senator John Sherman, and asked him to prevent any move that would make him Grant's superior. He also wrote to Grant saying that he would rather have him in command than anyone else and that he would "emphatically decline any commission calculated to bring us into rivalry."

Grant replied:

No one would be more pleased at your advancement than I, and if you should be placed in my position and I put subordinate...I would make the same exertions to support you that you have ever done to support me.

LESSON

Take pride in your subordinates' accomplishments and never be jealous of their success.

213. PROTECT AGAINST UNWANTED SOLICITATIONS

*T*HROUGHOUT THE WAR, GRANT WAS TROUBLED BY THE assemblage of hangers-on that accompanied the troops and tried to bilk them. After the capture of Atlanta, Sherman turned the city into a military encampment.

Sherman also very wisely prohibited the assembling of the army of sutlers [peddlers] and traders who always follow in the wake of an army in the field, if permitted to do so, from trading with the citizens and getting money of the soldiers for articles of but little use to them, and for which they are made to pay most exorbitant prices.

LESSON

Your people deserve protection against being solicited by salespeople and fund raisers. All such activities need to be limited and tightly controlled.

214. CHOOSE YOUR WORDS CAREFULLY

*G*RANT BELIEVED THAT "ALL TRADERS" WERE "A CURSE TO the army." He had earlier in the war attempted to ban Jewish traders and speculators from his department by issuing his infamous General Order No. 11 (December 17, 1862).

The Jews, as a class violating every regulation of trade established by the Treasury Department and also department orders, are hereby expelled from the department within twenty-four hours from the receipt of this order.

This order was quickly revoked by President Lincoln. As Halleck explained to Grant:

The President has no objection to your expelling...Jew peddlers, which I suppose, was the object of your order; but, as it...proscribed an entire religious class, some of whom are fighting in our ranks, the President deemed it necessary to revoke it.

Grant was troubled by the uproar over his order. Years later, he told a rabbi that during the war:

[There was not] time to handle things with kid gloves. But it was no ill feeling or a want of good feeling toward the Jews. If such complaints [about traders and speculators] would have been lodged against a dozen men each of whom wore a white cravat, a black broadcloth suit, beaver, or gold spectacles, I should probably have issued a similar order against men so dressed.

The rabbi's account of his interview with Grant was published in the *Chicago Tribune* in April 1885, three months before Grant's death.

In December 1862, Grant had issued an order that reeked of bigotry. As President, Grant advocated religious tolerance. Yet, in spite of his later actions in support of Jews, Grant was never able to completely dispel the impression created by what he referred to as "that obnoxious order." He still ended up being tainted by the ugly specter of antisemitism.

LESSON

You can't be too careful in your choice of words. Carelessly chosen, they can cause you and others embarrassment and grief. Be especially careful about making generalizations. You never want to be guilty of tarring a group of people with a brush that applies to only a few of them.

215. ANTICIPATE YOUR PEOPLES' NEEDS

*A*FTER CAPTURING ATLANTA, SHERMAN MADE HIS FAMOUS march through Georgia. When he reached the Atlantic coast, he established communications with the Union navy.

> *When Sherman had opened communication with the fleet he found there was a steamer, which I had forwarded to him, carrying his accumulated mails for his army, also supplies which I supposed he would be in need of.*

LESSON

A good manager anticipates the needs of his or her subordinates.

216. GIVE THEM THE CREDIT

 ${}_S$ THE UNION'S MASTER STRATEGIST, GRANT COULD rightfully claim some, maybe even all, of the credit for planning Sherman's march to the sea.

The question of who devised the plan of march from Atlanta to Savannah is easily answered; it was clearly Sherman, and to him also belongs the credit of its brilliant execution.

LESSON

Never hesitate to give your subordinates all the credit they deserve; the better part of it will rub off on you anyway.

217. PLAN FOR CONTINGENCIES

*A*FTER CAPTURING SAVANNAH (DECEMBER 21, 1864), Sherman turned his army north into the Carolinas.

I took the precaution to provide for Sherman's army, in case he should be forced to turn toward the sea coast...by forwarding supplies to every place where he was liable to have to make such a deflection from his projected march.

LESSON

It pays to plan for contingencies. If you don't, and things go sour, you'll lose valuable time looking for a way around your current difficulties.

218. CUT YOUR PEOPLE SOME SLACK

*I*N DECEMBER 1864, GENERAL BENJAMIN BUTLER TOOK command of an expedition to capture Fort Fisher, North Carolina.

> *General Butler conceived the idea that if a steamer loaded heavily with powder could be run up to near the shore under the fort and exploded, it would create great havoc and make the capture an easy matter. Admiral Porter, who was to command the naval squadron, seemed to fall in with the idea.... I had no confidence in the success of the scheme, and so expressed myself; but as no serious harm could come...I permitted it.*

LESSON

Give your people the latitude to try something new, even if you're not high on the idea, but only if the consequences of failure are minor.

219. THE USE OF NEW TECHNOLOGY

*T*HE EXPLODING POWDER BOAT IDEA WAS ONLY ONE OF MANY novel suggestions made to Grant to use technology to win the war.

This is a very suggestive age. Some people seem to think that an army can be whipped by waiting for rivers to freeze over, exploding powder at a distance, drowning out troops, or setting them to sneezing; but it will always be found in the end that the only way to whip an army is to go out and fight it.

LESSON

The cost-effective use of new technologies can give you a competitive advantage and help you to succeed. But technology is not a panacea. More often than not, the path to success will be the application of good management to the basics of your business.

220. DON'T HOLD A GRUDGE

*A*LTHOUGH THE ATTEMPT TO BLOW UP FORT FISHER failed, Admiral Porter was convinced that the fort could have been captured with the forces at his and General Butler's command. But Butler, hearing that Confederate reinforcements might be coming, refused to attack the fort, and instead withdrew his troops. Admiral Porter was furious.

Porter sent dispatches to the Navy Department in which he complained bitterly of having been abandoned by the army just when the fort was nearly in our possession.

Six years later, President Grant nominated Porter for the senior position in the navy. Porter's enemies, in an attempt to get Grant to withdraw his nomination, published a letter Porter had written after the initial failure to capture Fort Fisher. In it, Porter was highly critical of Grant's handling of the affair, especially of his allowing Butler to head the expedition. Although stung by this, Grant not only refused to withdraw Porter's nomination, he actively supported him through the Senate confirmation process.

LESSON

You need to be able to accept criticism, especially when it's justified. Don't hold grudges; they eat at your soul.

221. WHEN SOMETHING SMELLS FISHY

AFTER THE FAILURE OF THE INITIAL ATTEMPT TO CAPTURE Fort Fisher, Grant relieved General Butler of command. While the primary reason was Butler's demonstrated lack of military ability, Grant also felt that Butler's "administration of the affairs of his department" was a problem.

Grant ordered General Halleck to have an officer on the inspector-general's staff in Washington "report to me for special duty. I want to get in an official form some facts that I have learned."

LESSON

Don't hesitate to use your internal auditors to help you ferret out the truth when confronted with a situation that you sense may be rotten at the core. While you don't want to go off on witch hunts, it is better to check out a hunch that something isn't right than it is to wait until the problem surfaces.

$222.$ TREAT YOUR PEOPLE FAIRLY

A SUBSEQUENT EXPEDITION UNDER THE COMMAND OF General Alfred Terry did take the fort.

He [Terry] is a man who makes friends of those under him by his consideration of their wants and their dues.

LESSON

Good managers are considerate of their people and treat them fairly.

223. GREAT MANAGERS ARE NEVER SATISFIED

*N*EWS OF GENERAL THOMAS' DECISIVE VICTORY OVER Confederate General Hood's army in the battle of Nashville (December 15th and 16th, 1864) relieved Grant of his anxieties about a possible Confederate breakthrough to the Ohio River. He immediately sent Thomas a telegram congratulating him on his "splendid success," and at the same time, letting him know that more remained to be done.

Push the enemy now and give him no rest until he is entirely destroyed. Your army will cheerfully suffer many privations to break up Hood's army and render it useless for future operations.... Much is now expected.

Lincoln also sent Thomas a telegram congratulating him:

You have made a magnificent beginning. A grand consummation is within your easy reach. Do not let it slip.

LESSON

The truly great managers are never satisfied. They always want more.

224. SURPLUS TROOPS

*A*FTER HIS VICTORY IN THE BATTLE OF NASHVILLE, General Thomas, as Grant saw it, failed to vigorously pursue the retreating Confederates. After reviewing Thomas' rationale for halting the pursuit, Grant decided to reduce the number of troops under Thomas' command.

This [Thomas'] report...determined me to use his surplus troops elsewhere.

LESSON

If you have a manager who isn't effectively utilizing all the resources assigned to him or her, reassign those resources to other managers who will put them to better use.

11

ALWAYS
DO WHAT'S RIGHT

February – December 1865

Grant takes Petersburg and Richmond and pursues the retreating Confederate army to Appomattox. Foreseeing the need for a just and speedy reconciliation, he offers Lee generous terms for surrender. As the fighting ends, Grant forbids cheering because "the rebels are our countrymen again."

225. TRY TO SETTLE DISPUTES THROUGH NEGOTIATION

*O*N FEBRUARY 3, 1865, PRESIDENT LINCOLN MET WITH three high-ranking members of the Confederate government who had sought an interview with him for the purpose of entering into peace negotiations. While their meeting was unsuccessful, it would almost certainly not have occurred at all but for the intercession of Grant. Horace Porter recalled that the President had decided against meeting with the Confederates.

General Grant telegraphed the President that he thought the gentlemen were sincere in their desire to restore peace and union, and that it would have a bad effect if they went back without any expression from one who was in authority, and said he would feel sorry if Mr. Lincoln did not have an interview with them, or with some of them. This changed the President's mind.

When Grant sent that telegram he felt certain that his coming spring offensive would end in the destruction or capture of Lee's army and the death of the Confederacy, yet he pushed his superiors to consider a negotiated settlement to the war.

LESSON

Always try to settle disputes honorably through negotiation.

226. RECOGNIZE THE LIMITS OF YOUR AUTHORITY

WHILE GRANT WAS WILLING TO PUSH HIS SUPERIORS TO the negotiating table, he knew that his own authority did not extend to the making of peace. When Lee wrote to Grant in March to propose that the two of them meet to discuss how the war might be brought to a close, Grant forwarded Lee's letter to Secretary of War Stanton. After conferring with Lincoln, Stanton sent Grant the following instructions:

The President directs me to say to you that he wishes you to have no conference with General Lee unless it be for the capitulation of General Lee's army.... He instructs me to say that you are not to decide, discuss or confer upon any political question. Such questions the President holds in his own hands.

Grant responded that under no circumstances would he exceed his authority, "or in any way embarrass the government. It was because I had no right to meet General Lee on the subject proposed by him that I referred the matter for instructions."

LESSON

Recognize the limits of your authority. There is a point beyond which you cannot push the envelope. You can always suggest a course of action to your superiors, even if you cannot take action unilaterally.

227. THE VALUE OF SYMBOLS

AS THE WINTER OF 1865 CAME TO AN END, GRANT KEPT expecting Lee to abandon the defenses around Petersburg and Richmond. "I could not see how it was possible for the Confederates to hold out much longer."

There is no doubt that Richmond would have been evacuated much sooner than it was, if it had not been that it was the capital of the so-called Confederacy, and the fact of evacuating the capital would, of course, have had a very demoralizing effect upon the Confederate army. When it was evacuated...the Confederacy at once began to crumble and fade away.

LESSON

Never underestimate the importance of symbols.

228. MAKE SURE YOUR PEOPLE KNOW YOU WANT THEIR INPUT

GRANT FREQUENTLY ASKED HIS SUBORDINATES FOR THEIR input. He recalled that at his first meeting with General Butler, in April 1864, he had invited Butler's views on the upcoming campaign. But sometimes his subordinates were reluctant to offer unsolicited advice. Shortly before the battle of Five Forks, Virginia (April 1, 1865), one of Grant's staff officers "asked Sheridan to come in to see me and say to me what he had been saying to them."

Sheridan felt a little modest about giving his advice where it had not been asked; so one of my staff officers came in and...suggested that I send for him. I did so, and was glad to see the spirit of confidence with which he was imbued. Knowing as I did from experience, of what great value that feeling of confidence by a commander was, I determined to make a movement at once.

LESSON

You need input from your subordinates. When it isn't offered, you must solicit it. But it will be offered if your people believe that you are sincere when you say you welcome their comments and recommendations.

229. THE ORGANIZATION DOESN'T REVOLVE AROUND YOU

*G*RANT THOUGHT HIGHLY OF MAJOR GENERAL G. K. WARREN, and as late in the war as the battle of Spotsylvania, he was prepared to give Warren command of the Army of the Potomac should something happen to General Meade. But Grant came to recognize that Warren's management was fatally flawed.

> *When he received an order to do anything, it would at once occur to his mind how all the balance of the army should be engaged so as properly to co-operate with him. His ideas were generally good, but he would forget that the person giving him orders had thought of others at the time he had of him.*

LESSON

If you make the mistake of behaving as if whatever responsibility you've been given is always the organization's number one priority, and everyone else's activities revolve around yours, you will be so busy trying to tell everyone else what to do that you'll fail to get your own job done. Certainly, make suggestions whenever you see opportunities for improvement; but don't try to run the whole show.

230. IF DISTRACTED BY FEAR

*G*RANT ALSO RECOGNIZED ANOTHER DEFECT IN WARREN'S character that limited his usefulness.

He could see every danger at a glance before he had encountered it. He would not only make preparations to meet the danger which might occur, but he would inform his commanding officer what others should do.

LESSON

You should not cast a blind eye on potential difficulties, or fail to have plans to deal with them. Remember, however, that our worst misfortunes usually occur only in our imaginations. If you allow yourself to be distracted by fear, you will surely fail.

231. LEARN TO DELEGATE OR YOU'LL END UP WITH A SMALL COMMAND

*F*INALLY, GRANT CAME TO REALIZE THAT WARREN WAS unable to delegate responsibility to his subordinates.

> *When he did get ready to execute an order, after giving most intelligent instructions to division commanders, he would go in with one division, holding the others in reserve until he could superintend their movements in person also, forgetting that division commanders could execute an order without his presence. His difficulty was constitutional and beyond his control. He was an officer of superior ability, quick perceptions and personal courage to accomplish anything that could be done with a small command.*

LESSON

Those who don't learn to delegate will never be successful managers. There are effective first-line supervisors who do not delegate, but it is invariably a mistake to promote them to higher levels of management. You should only promote first-line supervisors who encourage and train their staff to act in their absence.

$232.$ A LEOPARD CAN'T CHANGE ITS SPOTS

*I*T WASN'T UNTIL APRIL 1865 THAT WARREN, WHO WAS THEN reporting to Sheridan, was removed from command.

> *I had sent a staff officer to General Sheridan...to say that as much as I liked General Warren, now was not a time when we could let our personal feelings for anyone stand in the way of success; and if his removal was necessary to success, not to hesitate. It was upon that authorization that Sheridan removed Warren. I was very sorry that it had been done, and regretted still more that I had not long before taken occasion to assign him to another field of duty.*

LESSON

If you have managers who are ineffective because of inherent character flaws, lose no time in replacing them. No matter how much you may like them personally, they are failing. Retaining them in positions for which they are not suited does a disservice to them and to the organization. Reassign them if you have suitable openings; if you don't, help them to find other jobs.

233. JOHNNIES COME LATELY

On April 3rd, Petersburg and Richmond were occupied by Union troops. Lincoln, who had been visiting Grant's headquarters, rode into Petersburg to congratulate his general.

Mr. Lincoln knew that it had been arranged for Sherman to join me...to co-operate in the destruction of Lee's army. I told him that I had been very anxious to have the Eastern armies vanquish their old enemy.... I said to him that if the Western [Sherman's] armies should be even upon the field, operating against Richmond and Lee, the credit would be given to them for the capture.

LESSON

As a manager, getting proper credit for your accomplishments is not something you should be concerned about. However, you have the responsibility to insure that the contributions of those who have labored long and hard on a project are not eclipsed by those who arrive late in the game. Also, when success is assured with the staff on hand, don't add additional resources. By doing so, you would demonstrate that last-minute lack of confidence that can be so demoralizing.

234. AVOID HUMILIATING YOUR SUBORDINATES

URING THE PURSUIT OF LEE'S ARMY FOLLOWING THE capture of Petersburg and Richmond, Grant came to the conclusion that General Meade had issued orders that, if followed, would give Lee the opportunity to escape. Grant immediately went to explain the situation in person, "reaching his [Meade's] headquarters about midnight."

I explained to Meade that we did not want to follow the enemy; we wanted to get ahead of him, and that his orders would allow the enemy to escape.... Meade changed his orders at once.

LESSON

If you need to overrule one of your subordinates, always try, even if it's inconvenient to do so, to explain the rationale for your decision face to face. You can avoid humiliating your subordinate by giving him or her the opportunity to change the decision.

235. THE BEST MEDICINE

ON APRIL 8TH, GRANT HAD A TERRIBLE HEADACHE.

I spent the night in bathing my feet in hot water and mustard, and putting mustard plaster on my wrists and the back part of my neck, hoping to be cured by morning.

The next morning an officer brought Grant a note from Lee requesting a meeting to discuss the terms of surrender.

When the officer reached me I was still suffering with the sick headache; but the instant I saw the contents of the note I was cured.

LESSON

Good news is wonderful medicine.

236. WHEN YOU HOLD ALL THE CARDS

*B*EFORE SURRENDERING FORT DONELSON, THE Confederate commander had written to Grant, suggesting an armistice and the appointment of commissioners to draw up terms for the capitulation of the fort. Grant's response was the famous, "No terms except an unconditional and immediate surrender can be accepted."

Three years later in the exchange of letters that led to Lee's surrender at Appomattox, Grant wrote:

Your note...asking the condition on which I will accept the surrender of the Army of Northern Virginia is just received. In reply I would say that, peace being my great desire, there is but one condition I would insist upon, namely: that the men and officers surrendered shall be disqualified for taking up arms again against the Government of the United States.

Later, when Lee and Grant met, and Grant began to write down the terms for surrender,

...the thought occurred to me that the officers had their own private horses and effects, which were important to them, but of no value to us; also that it would be an unnecessary humiliation to call upon them to deliver their side arms.

LESSON

When you hold all the cards, you can call the shots. But you don't need to rub their noses in it. Try to treat everyone with dignity and respect.

237. ETHICAL PRINCIPLES

ROBERT E. LEE SURRENDERED THE ARMY OF NORTHERN Virginia on April 9, 1865, but five more Confederate commanders would have to surrender before the war would finally end. The morning after Lee surrendered, he and Grant had a private conversation. Lee expressed "his earnest hope...that we would not be called upon to cause more loss and sacrifice of life."

I then suggested to General Lee that there was not a man in the Confederacy whose influence with the soldiery and the whole people was as great as his, and that if he would now advise the surrender of all the armies I had no doubt his advice would be followed with alacrity. But Lee said, that he could not do that without consulting the President [of the Confederacy] first. I knew there was no use to urge him to do anything against his ideas of what was right.

LESSON

Don't try to get people to do things that they believe run counter to their ethical principles, even if you have the best of reasons for wanting them to do so.

238. UNNECESSARY SUCCESSES

*T*WO DAYS AFTER LEE SURRENDERED, MOBILE, ALABAMA WAS occupied by Union troops after a fierce battle.

I had tried for more than two years to have an expedition sent against Mobile when its possession by us would have been of great advantage. It finally cost us lives to take it when its possession was of no importance, and when, if left alone, it would within a few days have fallen into our hands without any bloodshed whatever.

LESSON

There are few things so sad as a costly, unnecessary success.

239. GET WHAT YOU WANT

*G*RANT DID NOT MEET ABRAHAM LINCOLN UNTIL HE WAS called to Washington to become head of the Union armies. But in the final year of the war they got to know each other well. Grant was a great admirer of the President, and when Lincoln was assassinated, he felt a great sense of loss, both personally and for the nation, in the untimely death "of so good and great a man."

I knew his goodness of heart, his generosity, his yielding disposition, his desire to have everybody happy.

Grant also had seen Lincoln function as an effective executive and had the highest respect for the President's managerial skills.

Mr. Lincoln gained influence over men by making them feel it was a pleasure to serve him. He preferred yielding his own wish to gratify others, rather than to insist upon having his way. It distressed him to disappoint others. In matters of public duty, however, he had what he wished, but in the least offensive way.

LESSON

The truly great managers have a gentle demeanor and give the appearance of being open-minded and pliable. Still, they get what they want.

240. BLIND RAGE

$\mathcal{G}$RANT THOUGHT THAT ABRAHAM LINCOLN "WAS incontestably the greatest man" he had ever known. He felt that the day Lincoln was assassinated was "the darkest day" of his life. When he learned that Lincoln was dead, Grant lashed out in a blind rage. The general, who had told his troops not to cheer when Lee surrendered because "the rebels are our countrymen again," the man who would accept his party's nomination for the presidency with the words, "Let us have peace," and who would invite Robert E. Lee to the White House, was on April 15, 1865 in a vengeful mood. To General Ord, commanding in Richmond, he sent the following order:

> *Arrest J. A. Campbell, Mayor Mayo and the members of the old council of Richmond, who have not yet taken the oath of allegiance, and put them in Libby prison. Hold them guarded beyond the possibility of escape until further orders. Also arrest all paroled officers....*

Ord promptly replied:

> *The two citizens I have seen. They are old, nearly helpless, and I think incapable of harm. Lee and staff are in town among the paroled prisoners. Should I arrest them...I will risk my life that the present paroles will be kept, and if you will allow me to do so trust the people*

here who, I believe, are ignorant of the assassination, done I think by some insane Brutus with few accomplices.

Grant calmed down and withdrew his order.

LESSON

Never act in anger, no matter what the provocation. Delay is the best remedy for anger. Give yourself time to calm down and think it over. Otherwise, you're likely to act irrationally.

241. THE GAME NEVER ENDS

*O*N MAY 9TH, GRANT WROTE TO JULIA.

But a short thirty-five days ago we had a defiant enemy holding the South; today we are telegraphing, through their own operators, and over the wires which they controlled so short a time since, regarding dispositions for the capture of their pretended President and Cabinet. Management is all that is now required to secure complete peace.

LESSON

Management success is akin to achieving a first down in a football game, except that for managers there is no goal line, there are no touchdowns, and the game never ends. Each first down must be followed by another and another, ad infinitum. You can't rest on your laurels, and managers who think they can quickly find themselves on the slippery slope to failure.

242. CELEBRATE

*W*ITH THE WAR FINALLY OVER, THE NATION CELEBRATED.

> *On the 18th of May orders were issued by the adjutant-general for a grand review...of Sherman's and Meade's armies. The review commenced on the 23d and lasted two days.... The sight was varied and grand: nearly all day for two successive days, from the Capitol to the Treasury Building, could be seen a mass of orderly soldiers marching in columns of companies.*

LESSON

Celebrations aren't just for managers. Be sure you include everyone in the organization who contributed to the success you're celebrating.

$243.$ PERSONAL GLORY

GENERAL SHERIDAN WAS UNABLE TO ATTEND THE GRAND review of the armies. Grant had sent him to Texas with orders to station his troops along the Rio Grande and to be prepared to assist Juarez in driving Napoleon III's French army out of Mexico.

Grant was not an admirer of Napoleon I. While a cadet at West Point, he did not join the popular Napoleon Club, but he nevertheless "recognize[d] his great genius." Grant had no respect, however, for Napoleon III, who had tried to take advantage of the American Civil War to establish a puppet regime in Mexico. Grant felt that Napoleon III's Mexican adventure was motivated by a desire for personal glory.

[Napoleon III] was an imitator without genius or merit.... He tried to play the part of the first Napoleon, without the ability to sustain that role. He sought by new conquests to add to his empire and his glory, but the signal failure of his scheme of conquest was the precursor of his own overthrow.

LESSON

A manager whose primary motivation is a desire for personal acclaim is certain to fail.

244. A DEAL IS A DEAL

*I*N JUNE 1865, GENERAL LEE LEARNED THAT HE WAS TO BE indicted for treason. Believing that his indictment would be a violation of the surrender terms that he and Grant had signed at Appomattox, he wrote to Grant:

I had supposed that the officers and men of the Army of Northern Virginia were, by the terms of their surrender, protected by the United States Government from molestation as long as they conformed to its conditions.

Grant insisted that the indictment be quashed, which it was.

LESSON

Once you've made a deal, stick to it. Some organizations have a reputation for always trying to change the terms they've previously agreed to. Large companies sometimes behave as though their size entitles them to take unfair advantage of their smaller business partners. If the deal turns out to be more expensive or more lucrative than contemplated, they'll insist on changing the terms of the contract to their advantage. Honor your agreements and keep your word, so that others will want to do business with you.

245. THERE ARE NO UNIMPORTANT PEOPLE

*I*N JUNE, GRANT MADE A VISIT TO WEST POINT. WINFIELD
Scott, a hero of the War of 1812 and commander of the U. S.
forces in the Mexican war, was living at West Point in retirement.
Grant, the hero of the hour and unquestionably the most popular
man in the nation, called on and paid his respects to the seventy-
nine year-old former commanding general of the United States.

LESSON

Ulysses S. Grant was a gentleman, and the mark of a gentleman is
the courtesy and respect that he accords to those people who are
not or can no longer be of any practical use to him.

246. NEVER LOSE TOUCH

*W*HILE TRAVELING AFTER THE WAR, GRANT'S TRAIN stopped in a Midwestern town where there was to be a luncheon in his honor. Grant was met by a welcoming committee and a brass band. On the other side of the tracks was a small group of veterans in their old uniforms who, Grant correctly guessed, had been excluded from the official celebration because of their shabby appearance. When Grant left the train, he went immediately across the tracks to speak with the veterans.

LESSON

As a manager, you will rise on the sweat of other peoples' brows. Never lose touch with the people to whom you owe your success. They will always deserve your utmost consideration.

247. BE WARY OF JOURNALISTS

*G*RANT, LIKE MOST PUBLIC FIGURES, HAD HIS SHARE OF RUN-ins with members of the press.

After the war, during the summer of 1865, I traveled considerably through the North, and was everywhere met by large numbers of people.... Correspondents of the press were ever on hand to hear every word dropped, and were not always disposed to report correctly what did not confirm their preconceived notions, either about the conduct of the war or the individuals concerned in it.

LESSON

There are journalists who look to make the news rather than to report it. They are not above distorting the truth, and they do not keep confidences. Be wary in all your dealings with the media. Especially avoid making off-the-record remarks; they will invariably come back to haunt you.

248. MERGER, NOT CONQUEST

WITH THE END OF THE CIVIL WAR, THE PAINFUL TASK OF reconstruction began. Grant was "in favor of a speedy reconstruction on terms that would be the least humiliating to the people who had rebelled against their government."

> *The people who had been in rebellion must necessarily come back into the Union, and be incorporated as an integral part of the nation. Naturally the nearer they were placed to an equality with the people who had not rebelled, the more reconciled they would feel with their old antagonists, and the better citizens they would be from the beginning.*

LESSON

The best way to pull off a merger is for the acquiring organization's management to treat those who have been acquired as equals. If the process of merging the two organizations denigrates into a game of winners and losers, with the employees of the non-surviving entity being treated as second-class citizens, the process of building a unified organization will be severely hampered.

$249.$ ALWAYS DO WHAT'S RIGHT

IN DECEMBER 1865, WITH THE RATIFICATION OF THE thirteenth amendment to the Constitution, slavery was finally abolished.

In 1858, Grant had purchased from his father-in-law a young black man, William Jones. Less than a year later, at a time when he was severely strapped for cash, Ulysses S. Grant chose not to sell his slave, who would have brought a handsome price, but to give him his freedom. Since he owned Jones for so short a period of time, it is possible that Grant purchased him for the express purpose of setting him free. While we cannot be certain of his purpose, we know Grant had a wife and four young children to feed, he was broke, and he probably could have gotten fifteen hundred dollars by selling Jones.

LESSON

Grant believed that "the moment conscience leaves, physical strength will avail nothing, in the long run." Always do what's right. It is in your and your organization's best interest to give ethical considerations priority.

250. YOU CAN'T STOP THE CLOCK

*I*N HIS MEMOIRS, GRANT TOLD HIS LIFE STORY THROUGH THE end of the Civil War. He began writing his memoirs in the fall of 1884, when he already knew that he was dying of cancer. He finished writing the book the following May, but continued reviewing and making changes to the proofs until shortly before his death on July 23, 1885. Grant's memoirs are a masterpiece.

Grant himself was sorry that his failing health required him to complete the writing of his memoirs in a shorter time period than he would otherwise have devoted to the project.

I would have more hope of satisfying the expectation of the public if I could have allowed myself more time. I have used my best efforts...to verify from the records every statement of fact given. The comments are my own, and show how I saw the matters treated of whether others saw them in the same light or not.

LESSON

You are rarely given as much time as you would like to complete a project. Instead of complaining about unreasonable time frames, recognize that time constraints can be taken advantage of to force a remarkable concentration of effort that can produce impressive, and perhaps otherwise unachievable, results.

CONCLUSION

The Quintessential Grant

Ulysses S. Grant knew the right things to do. This chapter briefly summarizes the dozen overriding management principles he followed to get them done.

1. USE THE PLANNING PROCESS TO SET PRIORITIES

The purpose of the planning process is to identify, from among the myriad of things that could be done, those few strategic objectives that when achieved would produce previously unattainable results. The planning process is the vehicle for setting priorities. It is also the means by which new ideas, old beliefs, and current practices are put under the magnifying glass. Planning provides a strategic framework for action, but it doesn't end with the publication of the annual business plan. The process is dynamic and continuous. There is nothing sacrosanct about the individual goals or action plans that are developed. These may have to be modified, but if you use the planning process to set priorities, you'll continue to stay focused on achieving your objectives.

2. FOCUS ON THE CONTRIBUTION YOU COULD BE MAKING

Don't worry about the things you can't control. Instead, focus on what you could be doing to achieve your objectives. Don't get sidetracked into pursuing easy successes. You mustn't lose sight of your priorities. The yardstick you should use to measure your performance is not a list of minor accomplishments, no matter how long. Even extraordinary performance on a secondary priority is only an unnecessary success and an unwelcome distraction. The real measure is the contribution you are making toward achieving your primary objectives, and this is where you need to concentrate your efforts.

3. BE PERSISTENT AND TENACIOUS

Lincoln thought that Grant's greatest strength was his "dogged pertinacity." You will need persistence and tenacity to overcome the obstacles and setbacks you encounter. Action plans may need to be dropped, goals changed, or alternate plans developed, but you cannot shift your focus from achieving the key objectives that are critical to success.

4. IDENTIFY THE INFORMATION YOU NEED

Today's managers are inundated with data. Far too many of them allow themselves to become virtual prisoners of their data processing departments. They spend their days locked in their offices, chained to their personal computers or poring over printouts. You need to identify your critical information needs, that small subset of the detailed data that you must review in order to do your job effectively. Then you must discipline yourself to look only at that information. The demands on you, just in the way of meetings and special projects, are such that you don't have the time to look at anything else without becoming completely bogged down in petty details. If you are going to succeed you need to see for yourself what's happening, and to do that, you need to escape from your office, walk through the work areas, and talk to your staff.

5. CREATE A THINKING MACHINE

Grant believed that the best managers are the ones who create thinking machines. Hire individuals who are intelligent, eager to learn, show initiative, and have common sense. Help them to realize a shared sense of purpose through discussions of your objectives and the important role each of them plays in implementing the goals and action plans that lead to those objectives. Give them empowering instructions, but remember that empowered people make mistakes. Reinforce the empowerment message by turning those mistakes into training opportunities.

6. SURROUND YOURSELF WITH GOOD PEOPLE

You have no task more important than the selection and training of those who will do the work, and the most important selections of all are of those who will manage them. Surround yourself with honest, candid men and women who are not afraid to disagree with you, and make it clear that you want their input.

7. REMEMBER THAT THE WORK MUST BE DONE BY OTHERS

Never forget that you cannot succeed if the people working for you fail, so you must do everything possible to insure their success. This means giving them assignments that play to their strengths and following up to make sure the work is being done to your satisfaction. Also, recognize your own strengths and weaknesses, and don't hesitate to delegate those tasks that can be better performed by someone else. You need to delegate, because if you do their jobs you won't have time to do yours.

8. BE CONSIDERATE AND FAIR TO YOUR PEOPLE

The best way to retain good people and get them to work well together is to be consistent and evenhanded. It's counterproductive to be abusive or inconsiderate. Superior results are easier to attain when your people feel you treat them fairly and with consideration. Two obvious points to remember: First, you must be color- and gender-blind; performance is what matters. Second, you need to give credit and rewards to those who have earned them.

9. MAKE ALLIES OF THOSE WHO DON'T REPORT TO YOU

You need to create allies; otherwise you will be unable to tear down the fences in the organization. Without allies you will find it difficult, if not impossible, to make use of resources that don't directly report to you. You need to co-opt those whose support you need by making them your partners in every phase of activity, from initial planning to final implementation, and by sharing the credit for your success.

10. RECOGNIZE THAT SUCCESS IS TEMPORARY

Every success must be followed by another, and each time the bar is raised a little higher. There is the story of the chicken farmer who carries an ostrich egg into his hen house, claps his hands to get the hens' attention, and says, "Listen up. I'm not complaining, mind you, but this is just a sample of what the competition is doing." Even as you search for ways to shatter existing paradigms and take giant strides, you need to continue to set goals for incremental improvements. You can never afford to be satisfied or to let up.

11. ALWAYS ACT ETHICALLY

Once you give your word, keep it. Even if you've made a bad bargain, a deal is still a deal, and you should always honor your agreements. Being the most powerful party at the negotiating table doesn't give you the right to act like a bully. Treat the other party the way you would want to be treated were the situation reversed. Don't lie or tell half-truths. Liars end up believing their own lies, and this invariably causes them to fail, because you don't learn anything from lies. Admit your mistakes and take full responsibility for your actions. Never try to lay the blame on someone else. Don't claim more credit than you deserve. In short, hold yourself to the highest ethical standards.

12. TRUST YOURSELF TO MAKE GOOD DECISIONS

What Sherman most admired about Grant was his self-confidence. Good managers are decisive, and self-confidence is a prerequisite to decisiveness. Gather input before making a decision, but don't be afraid to act in the absence of consensus. Don't procrastinate. Waiting doesn't make the decision any easier, and if your staff sees that you lack a sense of urgency, they will slack off. Trust yourself to sift out the truth from among the different opinions and make the right decision.

THE NEED FOR VISION

Ulysses S. Grant's vision was for the United States to become "a nation of great power and intelligence" with "peace, happiness and prosperity at home, and the respect of other nations." For his vision to be realized, the Union had to be preserved. The leaders of the Confederacy had a different vision of the future. They foresaw a divided America and a greatly weakened United States. The Civil War was fought to determine which of these two visions would prevail. It was, as Grant wrote, "a very bloody and a very costly war. One side or the other had to yield principles they deemed dearer than life before it could be brought to an end." The outcome was in doubt right up until the final months of the war. Grant's single-mindedness of purpose, formidable management skills, and consistent application of his management principles brought him victory and set the United States on the path to greatness that he had envisioned.

Following Grant's management principles will help you to turn your vision into a reality, but first you must have a vision. Principles cannot be applied in a vacuum. You need to decide where you want to go before you can use Grant's principles to help you get there.

ADDENDUM

Grant's Mismanaged Presidency

If it would be possible in any way for me to make a sacrifice for the American people, I would like to repay them by some sacrifice for the great honors they have conferred on me.

Ulysses S. Grant, to James M. Comly, in March 1876

$\mathcal{T}$he ultimate sacrifice for Ulysses S. Grant was to accept his grateful nation's highest office. When he agreed to head the Republican ticket in 1868, Grant was a four-star general, the first American to achieve that rank. As such, he was guaranteed a lifetime job with an income that freed him from financial worries. He knew that if he left the army he would have to forfeit that security and face an uncertain financial future. After leaving the White House, he would be unemployed and without a source of income, since ex-presidents received no pension at that time. What Grant couldn't have known was how great his sacrifice would be. The presidency forever tarnished his reputation.

The popular conception is that Grant was a terrible president whose administration gave rise to one scandal after another. In recent years, Americans have witnessed a seemingly endless procession of scandals emanating from the White House and the executive branch of government. Public opinion polls indicate that, with the exception of Watergate, they have had little impact upon the popularity of the president on whose watch they occurred. I am not suggesting we should reevaluate Grant's scandal-ridden administration in light of the scandals that plagued Nixon, Clinton, or any other president. Grant's presidency is disappointing because Grant was a hero, and we expect more of our heroes than we do of mere politicians elected to high office. While Grant's eight years in the White House were not devoid of accomplishments, they fell far short of what we would have anticipated from the superb manager who won the Civil War.

An in-depth management study of Grant as President would require a separate volume. All I will do here is briefly highlight three of the important management lessons that General Grant taught, but that President Grant failed to apply.

CREATE ALLIES

Grant understood the importance of creating allies and as a general, he had made his naval counterparts full-fledged partners in his operations. Admiral Porter was the first person with whom he discussed his plans for the capture of Vicksburg, and without the wholehearted support and cooperation of the naval forces under Porter's command, Grant would never have taken Vicksburg.

The Constitution empowers the president to make Cabinet appointments and negotiate treaties "with the Advice and Consent of the Senate." With the solid majority he had in both houses of Congress, Grant could reasonably expect to get most of what he wanted. Yet Grant began his administration by naming his Cabinet without consulting the leaders of his party. This initial failure to create allies started his administration on a sour note and left a bad taste that lasted throughout his presidency.

Senators from his own Republican Party blocked Grant's first choice for Secretary of the Treasury, the brilliant businessman Alexander T. Stewart. Grant's presidency is blamed for the severe recession that followed the financial panic of 1873, much as Herbert Hoover's is for the stock market crash of 1929 and the Great Depression. It is intriguing to speculate about whether the recession that began in 1873 might have been averted had Stewart been heading the Treasury Department.

Grant's failure to create allies also deprived the United States of a foothold in the Caribbean. Grant proposed the construction of a canal across Central America and sent surveyors to the region to find a suitable site. He foresaw that, to the United States, "the benefits [would be] incalculable." To insure the security of the proposed canal, he negotiated a treaty for the peaceful annexation of the Dominican Republic. Senate ratification would have led to the establishment of a naval base and a permanent U.S. presence in the Caribbean, but Republican senators, smarting from not having been consulted, were instrumental in preventing ratification. Thirty years later, the U.S. would go to war with Spain to gain what Grant could have had without firing a shot.

Why didn't President Grant begin his administration by making allies of his party's leaders? Only forty-six years old when he was elected, the youngest man to hold the office until then, Grant was politically naive. Before his inauguration, he told one Republican delegation, "I am not the representative of a political party." Eight years later, in his final State of the Union message, a wiser and sadder President Grant would write, "It was my fortune, or misfortune, to be called to the office of the Chief Executive without any previous political training."

THE PLANNING PROCESS

Upon being given command of all the Union armies, Grant immediately began developing the planning framework that enabled him to win the war. General Grant demonstrated how the planning process could be used to focus all of an organization's energies on achieving the strategic objectives required to fulfill its mission.

In the presidential election of 1868, blacks had been allowed to vote in all of the Confederate states that had been readmitted to the Union, but in only eight of the other twenty-six states. Many white Northerners found it easy to champion equal rights for Southern blacks but were less than enthusiastic about racial equality in their own backyard.

One of President Grant's strategic objectives was to achieve racial equality, and he stated it clearly in his inaugural address: "security of person, property, and free religious and political opinion in every part of our common country." The Civil War had ended only four years before Grant set that objective, and the process of reconstructing the South had already been derailed as a result of the bitter battles between his predecessor, Andrew Johnson, and the Radical Republicans who controlled Congress. It would have taken all of Grant's considerable management skills to get Reconstruction back on track.

Grant began his presidency with the words that are inscribed on his tomb, "Let us have peace," but there was no peace during his administration. In the South, blacks were being terrorized and murdered. Grant sent troops into South Carolina to arrest Klansmen in 1871 and to protect black voters during the election of 1876. In 1874 he used the army to disperse White League militia, who had overthrown the Louisiana State government, and to stop the killing of blacks. In spite of Grant's efforts, the pre-war economic, political, and social order was being reestablished. Blacks were no longer slaves, but they would have to wait another hundred years before the promise of racial equality would begin to become a reality.

Some historians contend that it is unfair to criticize Grant for failing to heal the nation's Civil War wounds during his eight years as president, when we are still licking those same wounds today. Even William S. McFeely, whose biography of Grant is very critical of his presidency, writes, "If Ulysses Grant had had all the wit and wisdom in the world, it might not have been enough to bring eleven rebel states into line on Reconstruction."

From a management perspective, Grant failed to apply the planning process that he employed so successfully to win the Civil War. While even the best plans will not succeed if they are not well implemented, General Grant demonstrated that careful planning was the critical first step on the road to victory.

President Grant never developed any plans to achieve the racial equality he called for in his inaugural address. Without plans of his own to implement, he was powerless to take affirmative actions. Instead, he reacted to the spreading violence, stopping its worst excesses, winning a battle here and there, but in the end losing the war. By the end of his second term, his failure to use the planning process in the fight for racial equality had left him a sidelined spectator who could only watch with a sense of helplessness and frustration the continued subjugation of America's Southern blacks.

Given Grant's objective and his mastery of the planning process, his failure to take the initiative in the struggle to achieve equal treatment for black Americans is puzzling. I think the problem lay in Grant's view of the presidency. He couldn't conceive of using it as a bully pulpit to gain popular support for his policies. Instead, Grant believed that the President should "on all subjects have a policy to recommend, but none to enforce against the will of the people." Unfortunately, on the subject of racial equality, the United States was a deeply divided nation. The will of the people was anything but clear.

YOU NEED GOOD PEOPLE

General Grant knew the importance of having good people and getting them to work together as a team. His wartime subordinates included men of unquestioned integrity who had the courage to tell him when they thought he was making a mistake. Grant gave no special favors to friends or relatives, because in war picking the wrong person for a job costs lives, as does failing to follow up and make sure the work is done properly.

During President Grant's administration, an Assistant Treasurer of the United States had to resign after it was revealed that he had been involved, along with Grant's brother-in-law, in a conspiracy to corner the gold market. His first-term Vice President accepted a bribe in the Credit Mobilier scandal. An Attorney General and Secretaries of the Interior, Navy, Treasury, and War were all implicated in money-grubbing scandals, as was Grant's younger brother. Worst of all, the White House Chief of Staff stood trial for his involvement in the infamous Whiskey Ring scandal in which over one hundred people were convicted of defrauding the government.

Grant didn't invent the spoils system, but he did become a captive of it. Geoffrey Perret, in his biography of Grant, concludes that the series of scandals for which Grant's presidency is best remembered is a reflection of American politics at the time he took office: "Crookedness proliferated at every level of government. By 1869, parts of the Federal bureaucracy, much of Congress, and both national political parties, were sustained by corruption."

During an age when two future presidents of the United States, Chester A. Arthur and James A. Garfield, thought nothing of accepting bribes, and when political patronage determined who would receive the get-rich-quick positions of customs officials, tax collectors, and Indian agents, it isn't surprising that Grant's attempt to enact meaningful civil service reform fell on deaf ears in Congress. Nor was Grant the first or the last president to discover that some of the people he trusted couldn't resist the lure of easy riches that came with political power. The least that can be said is that unlike some presidents who have tried to cover up scandals in their administrations, he did not.

General Grant was closely acquainted with the men who served under him—not just the generals, but many of the other officers as well. President Grant was not. In his final State of the

Union message, Grant acknowledged that "in nearly every case" the people he appointed "were selected without personal acquaintance." With a candor lacking in most presidents, he admitted that he had made mistakes.

General Grant was knowledgeable in every facet of army operations, and expert in many. He was a hands-on manager, a master of detail, who got out and saw for himself what was happening in the units under his command. President Grant thought of himself as "a purely Administrative officer," more like a presiding magistrate than a manager. As a result, he allowed himself to be trapped in the White House and fed information filtered through his aides. No wonder he knew too few of the people serving in his administration and too little about what some of them were doing.

PRESIDENT GRANT'S ACCOMPLISHMENTS

Because of the scandals, Grant's presidency is often likened to that of Warren G. Harding's. Grant deserves better. Amos T. Akerman, who served as Grant's Attorney General, wrote of his administration, "its merits are in primary things, its faults in trivial things." Akerman's assessment, made before the end of Grant's first term, was premature, but not totally wrong. While Grant's performance as president was not equal to that of Grant the general, he still could point with pride to a number of accomplishments:

- Ratification of the Fifteenth Amendment to the Constitution, which states that the right to vote shall not be denied "on account of race, color, or previous condition of servitude"

- Passage of civil rights enforcement legislation

- Creation of the Department of Justice and the post of Solicitor General of the United States

- Prosecution of the Ku Klux Klan

- Creation of the first Civil Service Board

- Appointment of the first Native American to be Commissioner of Indian Affairs

- Creation of the first Board of Indian Commissioners

- Implementation of Grant's Peace Policy, in which he called for the "civilization and ultimate citizenship" of the "original occupants of this land—the Indians"

- Peaceful settlement of Civil War related claims and boundary and fishing rights disputes with Great Britain, when war was a very real possibility

- Reduction of the national debt and return to specie-backed currency

- Creation of the world's first national park, Yellowstone

Grant won reelection in 1872 with a greater popular margin than he had received in 1868. He would in all likelihood have been reelected for a third term had he chosen to run again. On the day Grant left office, James A. Garfield wrote in his diary, "No American has carried greater fame out of the White House than this silent man who leaves it today."

INDEX

Fund raisers, protecting against, 250
Future, planning for, 23

G

Gift horses, 59
Good news, as medicine, 275
Good people, attracting/retaining, 195, 297, 307-9
Granger, Gordon, 100
Grant, Julia Dent, 24, 28, 46, 282
Grant, Ulysses S.:
   at Fort Donelson, 55, 57, 59, 60, 62, 63, 103
   command of the Army of the Potomac, 151
   death of, 291
   early childhood, 3, 5
   farming experience, 28
   and Illinois infantry regiment, 36-37
   marriage of, 24
   memoirs of, 291
   Mexican war experiences, 14-19, 55
   and the press, 288
   promotion to lieutenant general, 195
   real estate experience, 28
   and reconstruction, 289
   Shiloh (Tennessee), battle of, 69-81
   and slavery, 290
   Vicksburg campaign, 121-23, 126-29, 147-51

West Point era, 3, 6-8, 55, 284
Grudges, holding, 258

H

Halleck, Henry W., 40, 64, 65, 80, 85, 87, 88, 92-95, 135, 152, 163, 198, 222, 229, 251, 259
Hamer, Thomas, 23
Hardee, William, 40
Harris, Thomas, 41
Hays, Alexander, 214
Help, giving assurance of, 171
Holding grudges, 258
Holly Springs supply base, 121
Hood, John Bell, 189, 247
Hooker, Joseph, 175, 182
Hovey, Alvin, 124
Humanity, retaining, 69
Humiliation of subordinates, 274
Humor, 61
Hunches, following, 259
Hunter, David, 241

I

Identifying information needed, 296
Impossible assignments, 20
Inadequate information, 124
Ineffective managers, replacing, 272
Inexperienced managers, 44